Glue

Sticking Power for Lifelong Marriages

PAUL AND PATTI ENDREI

VIP
VISION IMPRINTS PUBLISHING
A Thomas Nelson Company

www.thomasnelson.com
Tulsa, Oklahoma

GLUE
© 2006 by Paul and Patti Endrei

Published by Vision Imprints Publishing, Inc.
8801 S. Yale, Suite 410
Tulsa, OK 74137
918-493-1718

ISBN 1-599510-11-1
Library of Congress catalog card number: 2005938987

Printed in the United States of America

ENDORSEMENTS

"Glue is a priceless resource equipping you with practical tools needed for a successful marriage. With humorous anecdotes, Paul and Patti Endrei give you straightforward insight into the heart of a husband and a wife. This is not only a great 'how-to' for couples but a call to enhance every area of your marriage."
— John Bevere
   Author, Speaker
   President of Messenger International
   Colorado, Australia, United Kingdom

"Glue is practical, easy to read relationship advice from Paul and Patti Endrei who walk out these principles in their own lives. Whether a couple is just starting to get it together or they're putting it back together, *Glue* will help any couple keep it together."
— Dr. Leo and Molly Godzich
   Founders of NAME—National Association
   of Marriage Enhancement
   Marriage Pastors
   Phoenix First Assembly

"Paul and Patti capture the true underpinnings of what brings intimacy to a marriage relationship in *Glue*. At the foundation, and you can see it subtly woven throughout every chapter, is the idea of character—how we treat one another."
— Ken Blackwell
   Ohio Secretary of State

DEDICATION

We dedicate this book to our parents who have been married, as of the writing of this book, a combined ninety-three years (Paul's parents, forty-nine years and Patti's parents, forty-four years) to the same spouses! Frank and Ardelis Endrei and Bob and Dottie Spartz, you have provided us and the world with the templates for lifelong marriages! May God bless you with many more happy years of "sticking together." We, and your eleven grandchildren, are forever grateful.

We also dedicate this book to Dr. Louis and Tina Kayatin, our dear friends and lifelong ministry partners. Your model marriage has given us and our generation hope and help to make it to the marital finish line and to enjoy every bit of the journey! Your love for God and each other is contagious.

Paul and Patti Endrei

CONTENTS

Foreword
Acknowledgements

MEN STICKING RELATIONALLY
ℬℭ

Chapter One
Love Her Children and Treat Them Well
19

Chapter Two
Compliment Her Publicly and Privately
25

Chapter Three
Give Her Your Full Attention When She's Talking to You
31

Chapter Four
Control Yourself When She Makes a Mistake
35

Chapter Five
Be a Gentleman
41

Chapter Six
Pamper Your Wife
47

WOMEN STICKING RELATIONALLY
ℬℭ

Chapter Seven
Learn to Fight Fairly
53

Chapter Eight
Don't Correct Him in Public
59

Chapter Nine
Don't Nag
63

Chapter Ten
Romancing Romeo
69

Chapter Eleven
Don't Replace Your Husband with the Kids
73

MEN STICKING PRACTICALLY

ഇറ

Chapter Twelve
Be Her Superhero
81

Chapter Thirteen
Help Around the House
87

Chapter Fourteen
Gift Giving
93

Chapter Fifteen
The Ultimate Act of Love
101

Chapter Sixteen
Bedroom Etiquette
105

WOMEN STICKING PRACTICALLY
℘℃

Chapter Seventeen
Give Him a She-Mote Control
111

Chapter Eighteen
Home "Reentry"
115

Chapter Nineteen
Learn the Art of Timing
121

Chapter Twenty
Tell Him What You Really Want
127

Chapter Twenty-One
Make a Good Report List
131

Chapter Twenty-Two
Keep Improving Yourself
137

MEN STICKING EMOTIONALLY
℘℃

Chapter Twenty-Three
Make Her Laugh
143

Chapter Twenty-Four
Surprise, Surprise, Surprise
147

Chapter Twenty-Five
Build up Her Self-Esteem
153

Chapter Twenty-Six
Fulfill Her Emotional Needs
157

WOMEN STICKING EMOTIONALLY
ഇൻൻ

Chapter Twenty-Seven
Be His Number One Cheerleader
165

Chapter Twenty-Eight
Appreciate Your Husband's God-Given Personality
171

Chapter Twenty-Nine
Be a Woman He Can Share His TNT With
175

MEN STICKING SEXUALLY
ഇൻൻ

Chapter Thirty
Eyes Only for Her
181

Chapter Thirty-One
Nonsexual Touching
185

Chapter Thirty-Two
Romeo, Romeo—Where Art Thou?
191

Chapter Thirty-Three
Don't Be a Deadhead after Sex
197

WOMEN STICKING SEXUALLY
ഉറ

Chapter Thirty-Four
Don't Make Your Husband Beg for Sex
203

Chapter Thirty-Five
Are Men Shallow?
207

Chapter Thirty-Six
Have Sex with Your Husband More Than Once a Week
211

Chapter Thirty-Seven
Initiate Sex with Your Husband
215

Chapter Thirty-Eight
Let Him Know That You Enjoy Having Sex with Him
219

MEN STICKING SPIRITUALLY
ഉറ

Chapter Thirty-Nine
Lay Hands on Her and Pray for Her
227

Chapter Forty
Start a Storehouse
231

WOMEN STICKING SPIRITUALLY
ഓൽ

Chapter Forty-One
Marry His Dream
237

Chapter Forty-Two
Pray for Your Husband
243

About the Authors

FOREWORD

We sat down to write a marriage book for real people who want to do life together rather than separately. It's true that one can be in a crowded party and feel lonely. The truth is, there are many lonely husbands and wives in marriages today feeling about as "left out" as a ham sandwich at a Bar Mitzvah! Whether you're feeling "left out in the cold" in your marriage or just want a marriage booster shot, this "nuts-and-bolts" book is for you!

These real-life love stories will make you laugh at us and with us as we consider the dumb things we all do from time to time in this most challenging of all relationships, marriage. Marriage may be made in heaven, but it's got to be lived out down here on earth. As we let down our hair and "tell it like it is," it's our prayer that you will be encouraged to not just survive but thrive in your marriage. As a marriage building team, we have seen many marriages overcome miscommunication, hurts, hardships, bad habits, and infidelity. You can make it!

Though women purchase and read approximately 80 percent of marriage books, *Glue* is not just another marriage book for women. This book is made for men as well. The chapters are short and we give plenty of attention to sex! It's our desire that both husbands and wives will better understand their spouses through the forty-two, fun-filled, fast reading chapters that speak to the heart of many marriage issues.

Glue will give you the foundational habits and staying power needed to make your marriage stick together for a lifetime.

It is our purpose and passion to help you connect or reconnect with your soul mate so that you can experience the abundant life in a triple cord marriage of body, soul, and spirit.

Pastor Paul and Patti Endrei

ACKNOWLEDGEMENTS

We are so very grateful to our staff at Church On the Rise who have risen to the challenge of assisting us with this book. Connie Lindemann, your input, over-sight and constant creativity are second to none! We couldn't have done it without you. Christie Hess, you have been such a blessing in transcribing my hand-writing and doing all of the typing for this, our first book. Honor is also due to our pastoral staff who "sacrificially" helped brainstorm, on the beach for a week, in North Carolina! Jim and Jennifer Wilkes, your help with the "sticking points" and follow through was invaluable. Jeff Ballard, your photos always make us look better than life! Teri Gonska, your contributions made this project flow much smoother. Thank you, Church On the Rise Family, for your prayers and support from start to finish! And finally, we want to thank our Heavenly Father for being the Superglue in our twenty-three-plus years of marriage!

MEN
STICKING RELATIONALLY

CHAPTER ONE

Love Her Children and Treat Them Well

*Fathers, do not exasperate your children;
instead, bring them up in the training
and instruction of the Lord.*

Ephesians 6:4 (NIV)

A woman's most basic needs are primarily met through close intimate relationships. She longs for security and for a healthy, happy family. I have often told men dating single moms that it is imperative that they get along with and love her children. I have actually seen marriages break up because the new husband couldn't have a relationship with her children, even though they had a good relationship with each other as husband and wife.

You cannot separate a woman from her kids and you will pay a great price if you attempt it. One of the quickest ways to show your love for your wife is through her children.

What a Wife Desires for Her Children:

1. She wants her husband to be patient with them.

She's not looking for an Archie Bunker who called his son-in-law "meathead" and bad mouthed the rest of the family. A husband needs to think and speak positively about the kids, both privately and publicly.

2. Play with the kids, never ignore them.
Even when we are busy we need to at least greet, hug, and be warm with our children. Designate part of your family time to simply playing with the children. The family that prays together and plays together stays together. I find myself often on the ground with three of my younger children playing horsy as they pile on my back. They also like to be thrown on the bed or on the couch on a stack of pillows. Warning: Don't play too rough and hurt the kids, as this will put you in the penalty box for sure! As children grow older, their idea of playing is different. For my oldest son, it's playing golf and playing the market as we buy and sell stock together online.

3. Be a good example for them!
We have too many parole models and not enough role models in society today. Your wife wants a dad for her kids who sets an example worth following. God has designated the husband to be the point man and leader in the home. We need to lead by example more than anything else. Ask yourself, "How could I make changes in my life to provide a better example for my kids as spiritual leader, servant leader, and a good provider and protector of the family?"

ℬↃↄℛ
YOUR WIFE WANTS A DAD FOR HER KIDS WHO SETS AN EXAMPLE WORTH FOLLOWING.

4. Believe in them!

    God saw Gideon through the eyes of faith. God did not call him a miserable wimp but a mighty warrior. This is how we as fathers are to see our children. I don't look at my children for what they currently are but for what they will become in the future. Dads, we need to have patience and see them as God sees them, by focusing on the end result. Most drivers' training manuals will tell you that the best way to stay straight while driving on the highway is not to look directly across the front hood of the car but to look at a fixed point down the road. Keep your eyes focused on where you want to go with your children and be patient in the process.

5. Provide training for her children.

    Proverbs 22:6 (NIV) says, "Train a child in the way he should go, and when he is old he will not turn from it." Fathers are to be the primary trainers of the children in the home. Instead, many are simply providing a roof over their heads and food on the table. Many times we fathers provide food and clothing for our children and leave the training to our wives. The Bible says that we are to "train up a child in the way he should go." That simply means that we train up our children according to their individual bents in life. Every child is bent with certain gifts and talents from birth. It is our job as fathers to help our children discover, develop, and explore those gifts. Dads, we are life coaches for our children. We need to spend the majority of our time sharing biblical principles of success rather than blowing the whistle when our children make mistakes.

Remember, you are loving your wife indirectly when you love and care for her children. In some cases, what you do or don't do for her children is even more important than what you do for her! This is one area that you cannot afford to neglect and one that will make your marriage happier and help you leave a positive legacy.

STICKING POINTS

❖ Rate yourself below on a scale of 1-10 on the five areas that a wife wants for her kids. Which area is your strength and which one is your weakness?

1. Be patient with them._____
2. Play with them, never ignore them._____
3. Be a good example for them._____
4. Believe in them_____
5. Provide training for them._____

❖ List at least two ways you can improve.
1._____
2._____

Compliment Her Publicly and Privately

Words satisfy the mind as much as fruit does the stomach; good talk is as gratifying as a good harvest.

Proverbs 18:20 (The Message)

One of the worst things you can do is fail to take notice of your wife when she takes the time to look good for you. It's important for a wife to feel that she is attractive to her husband. It is often better to say nothing than to say something negative or attempt to be subtle. For instance, when my wife is not wearing makeup I will sometimes squint my eyes, look at her, and say, "Do you have makeup on?" She is very well aware that she does not have makeup on and knows that I am also aware of that fact. Trust me, this does not create marital bliss. I have learned to go out of my way to compliment Patti when she dresses up, is wearing a new outfit, or has a new hairstyle. I don't only compliment her when we are alone, I also compliment her in public.

On one occasion, I was preaching in front of our entire congregation and told the people to turn to a certain Scripture. As they were looking in their Bibles, I was looking at my wife on the front row and she was looking fine. My eyes were bugging out of my head, my heart was pounding, my hands were sweating, and I totally lost my place in the Scriptures. I was mesmerized. I told everyone that I had looked at my wife while they were turning to the Scripture, and she looked so beautiful that I totally lost my place and needed someone to tell me which Scripture I had just asked everyone to turn to. The congregation roared with laughter and I slowly but surely regained my place in the message.

I always want to be transparent about my marriage and my feelings toward my wife. I am not simply going to compliment Patti privately, but I am willing to let others know how much she means to me and how beautiful she is. This does two things to enrich my marriage. First of all, it makes my wife feel great and secure in our marriage. Secondly, it makes a very clear statement to any person who would try to come between us that we have a strong love for each other and that we have affair-proofed our marriage.

A woman does not simply want to be recognized as an object of beauty. Husbands, there are many other assets you can find to compliment your wife on: her work accomplishments, her decorating skills in the house, her care of the children, her support of you, her wisdom in business decisions, her cooking and management of the household, et cetera. Both Patti and I have siblings who have gone through divorces because their spouses constantly criticized them in private. Criticism tears down a person and tears apart a relationship. Words are seeds that will create either death or life in a marriage or in any relationship. If your wife sees you complimenting her publicly yet criticizing her privately, she will think that you are either trying to show off or trying to impress others as to what a nice guy you are. When you only compliment her in private but never in front of others, she may conclude that you are embarrassed of her and that your private feelings and expressions are insincere. Remember also, your children are watching how you compliment your wife both publicly and privately. They will emulate you one day.

As a young married man, I made some major mistakes in regard to my public praise of my wife. I would privately praise her; but from time to time, publicly, I had a bad habit of making Patti the punch line of my jokes. Everyone would laugh but Patti. I noticed that she detached herself at times like that and when I got home, I would hear how hurt she was by my comments. I have talked to many women who have felt the very same pain of being made fun of by their husbands in public. Women want to be publicly cherished, not diminished. They don't need to be reminded of past failures or mistakes when you are out among friends and family. I remember being in a grocery store shopping one day when a man I knew came up to the checkout counter with his wife. During our conversation, he was constantly making her the punch line of his jokes and I remember him saying, "My wife thinks I'm a Greek god. She offers me burnt offerings every day." Sad to say, that man was divorced within two years.

When Patti and I got married we moved to my hometown, Cleveland, Ohio. Patti was now living far away from her parents. She was in a new marriage and a new ministry. She wanted desperately to make a good impression upon my family, who lived nearby. One day we got into an argument and I called my mother to complain. This almost started World War III. Patti was devastated and I left our apartment in a huff, staying away for hours. Fortunately, my mother did not take my side. She told me to work things out with Patti. It is very important that when you are speaking to your parents or to your friends about your wife, you speak positively about her. The Scriptures talk about the fact that two have become one. When you talk negatively about your wife, you make yourself look bad and bring distress and distrust into your marriage. Work your problems out between the two of you; don't invite division into your home and relationship. The "leave and cleave principal" of Genesis 2:24 (NKJV) says, "Therefore a man shall leave his father and mother and be joined to his wife, and they shall become one flesh." In-laws can quickly become outlaws when we speak evil about our spouses. By implementing biblical principles and professional counseling, mature married partners work out their personal problems through prayer, not through complaining about their spouse to their family and friends. A good question to ask is, "How do others perceive my marriage?" We all need to do some marital "P.R." work.

Psychologists tell us that it takes four positive statements to offset one negative statement and a healthy marriage will need to have seven positive comments to one negative comment. Often in marriage we do not have the proper ratio of positive to negative statements. Consider your ratio. Take a day to simply track the positive and negative statements that you make to and about your spouse. A four-to-one ratio is just simply maintaining your marriage and when you have less than four-to-one you are undermining your marriage.

Your wife is a mirror of your treatment toward her. She is a reflection of how you have treated her, not only physically, but mentally and verbally. If she is constantly depressed, discouraged, and feels down trodden, it is very likely that you have been knocking her down instead of lifting her up.

> ℘℃ℜ
> YOUR WIFE IS A MIRROR OF YOUR TREATMENT TOWARD HER.

If you don't want sparks to fly in your marriage and want to keep the home fires burning, be careful to do "P.R." work on your marriage through speaking praise-filled words to your wife, privately as well as publicly, especially among family, friends, coworkers, and even among strangers.

STICKING POINTS

❖ Stop, think, and rate how well you praise your wife publicly and privately on a scale from 1-10, with 10 being the highest. How would you rate yourself?

❖ It is easy to take your wife for granted. Ask yourself if you overlook your wife's strengths and contributions. This week compliment her each day privately and publicly.

CHAPTER THREE

Give Her Your Full Attention
When She's Talking to You

I'll give you my full attention: I'll make sure you prosper,
make sure you grow in numbers, and keep
my covenant with you in good working order.

Leviticus 26:9 (The Message)

Give your wife your full attention when she's talking to you. I am not good at this but I'm getting better. Like most men, my problem is that I can listen to my wife while intently watching the football game or while I am reading a business newspaper or even listening to my voice-mail messages from work. Patti hates it when I am on the phone listening to my twenty voice mails while she is trying to tell me the details of her day.

I am a multi-tasking kind of guy. I need to hang up the phone, put down the newspaper, turn off the TV, look her in the eyes, and at least *pretend* to make an effort to listen more intently. Right? Wrong! This is a common area where men fall short. We *pretend* to be listening but our minds are a thousand miles away. Our wives can see through our glazed eyes when we just pretend to be good listeners.

Remember, your wife wants to talk much more than you do. Statisticians say that the average woman speaks some twenty-five thousand words per day. If she has to get her twenty-five-thousand-word quota in every day, it is very important for you to become a good, attentive listener.

I have a businessman friend in our church who told me that he took another businessman out for a round of golf. He was on the cell phone much of the round until my friend literally lost his temper and told him, "If we are ever going golfing together again, you need to be off the cell phone!" If we can exasperate our friends and business partners with such behavior, just think how hurtful it must be to our spouses.

I recently had a couple in my office for marital counseling who are on the brink of divorce. The husband complained that his wife never turns her cell phone off and even takes calls during family dinner. He said he would be happily married if he could just get as much attention as her cell phone.

> ∞CR
> WIVES CAN INSTINCTIVELY TELL WHEN HUSBANDS ARE PRETENDING TO BE LISTENING.

One wife, on a vacation with her husband, admitted that she wanted to throw her husband's cell phone into the swimming pool and drown it. Cell phones are just one area where husbands often drop the ball.

Wives can instinctively tell when husbands are pretending to be listening and so they often will ask specific questions to see how much of their message has been missed. A good listener will "mirror back" what he is hearing often so that communication is clearly taking place. Communication is not complete until it is responded to, just like a phone call is not complete until someone answers on the other end. When you properly respond to what she is saying, you show that you care about her and that you are living with her in an understanding way.

The Bible actually instructs husbands in 1 Peter 3:7 (NKJV) to "dwell with them with understanding, giving honor to the wife." A man who readily listens to and experiences deep sharing of feelings with his wife is like a "trophy husband" to his wife. She will brag about you to others and show you off to her friends if you are a strong, sensitive communicator. Relationships are two-way streets, and likewise, communication needs to be two-way to be effective and make her feel honored and cherished.

STICKING POINTS

❖ Does your wife have your full attention when she is talking to you? If you asked her, how would she answer this question?

❖ Name three things you can personally do to show her you are listening. (Turn the cell phone off, maintain eye contact, et cetera.)

1._____

2._____

3._____

CHAPTER FOUR

Control Yourself When She Makes a Mistake

A gentle response defuses anger,
but a sharp tongue kindles a temper-fire.

Proverbs 15:1 (The Message)

A woman's car was sideswiped on a trip to the store. Tearfully opening the glove compartment, she found the insurance papers. Fumbling through them, she saw a note her husband had written. It read: "Dear Mary, when you need these papers remember, it's you I love, not the car." What an example of love this husband is for all of us! Most of the time when our wives make mistakes, they feel bad enough already and do not need reprimanding.

Some friends of ours had a situation that would test even the strongest of marriages. My friend, Dave, really takes good care of his cars. He had just finished cleaning up his new car and was getting ready to go out for the evening on a date with his wife, Connie. While waiting for Dave, Connie decided to move her car so her son could back out of the driveway easily as he was also leaving soon. She waited on the street for her son to back his car out. Instead, her son got out of his car and went back into the house. Her son went in and out of the house several times while Connie waited in the street. Impatient, Connie pulled back into the driveway behind her son's car. She hastily put her car into park and jumped out, ready to give her son a piece of her mind. By this time, Dave was outside just in time to see her car mysteriously pop out of park and start rolling down the driveway. Connie had left the driver's side door open on her car so it sideswiped Dave's brand new car as it rolled down the driveway. Dave ran after the rolling car and was able to hop into it just before it hit another car parked on the street. One friend commiserating with Dave over his wife's mistake said, "In eight seconds she wiped out two cars!"

Though I have numerous tales to tell about Patti's mishaps, they pale in comparison to the number of things I've done wrong over the years. When she does make a mistake, how I've learned to respond to them has made all the difference in our relationship.

One day before a major family vacation, my son Jordan and I put a large cargo carrier on top of our minivan. Later that day, my wife and our two-year-old daughter went to purchase some last minute items so we could finish packing.

When she returned home, Patti noticed that our neighbors were having a large party with about forty people in their yard. She was intrigued because after living next door to our neighbors for three years, she had never noticed them hosting a party before. Forgetting about the cargo rack, she proceeded to pull the van inside the garage. As she attempted to enter the garage, she heard a loud noise, the cargo rack scraped against the frame of the garage. She immediately stopped the van and looked out her rear view mirror to see forty people gawking at her.

Knowing she couldn't leave the van parked halfway inside the garage, she put the van in reverse and once again heard the same loud screeching sound as the van became dislodged from the garage. She contemplated staying in the van until the forty people left the party but knew that no one was leaving until she got out. As she was about to exit the van and face the music, our daughter, Promise, said, "I'm not getting out, all those people are looking at us!"

After Patti mangled the cargo carrier and was totally embarrassed by the neighbor's onlooking guests, I just couldn't get angry. She thought I would get angry but it was so funny that all I could do was laugh. After I stopped laughing, I empathized with her and told her that I felt bad for her, which is what I should have done without laughing at her! I bent the cargo carrier back into shape as best as I could so we could go on vacation; and after our trip, I went out and bought an even bigger and better carrier.

The more recent blooper was soon after we moved into our new house. For many years we had sacrificed by buying fixer-upper houses, renovating and selling them for a profit. Patti and I have lived in ten different houses in our twenty years of marriage. Most of them we lived in while we fixed them up.

Finally, we were able to build our dream house. One day while Patti was busy doing household chores, our two-year-old son, Gideon, was begging her to play with him. She turned on the water in the laundry tub (on the second floor) to soak some clothes. As she rushed through her household chores, she completely forgot about the water being on. Ten minutes later, as she was changing Gideon's diaper beneath the laundry room, she felt water dripping on her face. She thought it was Gideon "anointing" her until she realized that the water was falling on top of her head. She looked up to see water pouring from the ceiling and even coming out of the light fixture! It took her only seconds to realize that she had forgotten to turn off the water in the laundry tub upstairs, but by then it was too late. The damage was done.

While all this was going on, I was on the phone with a leader from our church when I saw my two-year-old son running around the house with a dirty bottom and no diaper on. Patti started shouting and the baby was running around leaving an awful aroma. I quickly ended my conversation. When I came into the family room, I saw water pouring not only from the second floor ceiling but from Patti's eyes as well.

By now, the water, going through the first floor ceiling already, had also destroyed the ceiling tiles in the basement. Puddles were collecting all over the new carpet in the basement. After making sure the water was off, I excitedly asked Patti, "What happened here? How did this happen?" Patti was devastated, not by my questions but by what she inadvertently had done. I held her and told her I loved her. I wanted to assure her as I was leaving for a ten-day missions trip to Ethiopia and I didn't want to leave with a big wedge between us. I made a quality decision to forgive Patti and did my best to help clean up the mess. I then called the builder of the house to assess the damage.

When your wife makes a costly mistake or blunder what will make her love you more than ever is if you don't condemn her. Help her fix the problem as though it were your own. Situations like these are perfect opportunities to apply the golden rule. The Bible teaches us that, "Blessed are the merciful, for they will be shown mercy" (Matthew 5:7 NIV). The law of averages is against you. Chances are you will make some big blunders yourself and you will do well to sow seeds of mercy in your marriage.

> ℅℈℆
>
> **HELP HER FIX THE PROBLEM AS THOUGH IT WERE YOUR OWN.**

I have found that when my wife makes her biggest mistakes, responding with patience and love strengthens our relationship. 1 Corinthians 13 (NIV) is called the *Love Chapter* in the Bible, and the definition of love starts off with the simple phrase, "Love is patient, love is kind" (1 Corinthians 13:4). If God defines the foundations of love as expressing patience and kindness, then we should perceive such "trying times" as teachable moments for us to live in love and grow in grace.

STICKING POINTS

❖ Before a "trying time" occurs, take some time and plan how you will respond in a positive manner.

❖ Thinking back on her past blunders—how could you have responded differently?

CHAPTER FIVE

Be a Gentleman

Mark the perfect man, and behold the upright:
for the end of that man is peace.

Psalm 37:37 (KJV)

There is a story about a time when President McKinley had to make a difficult choice between two qualified men for a key position. An experience he had with one of the candidates helped him choose. One night, McKinley boarded a crowded streetcar. One of the two men being considered for the job was on it. An old lady with a heavy burden struggled to get on. The job candidate pretended he didn't see her and kept his seat. McKinley stood up and gave his seat to her. That man's lack of kindness cost him the job with the president.

Being a gentleman is never inappropriate or out of date. In fact, when you are out with your wife be extra careful to open doors for her, slide out her chair at restaurants, and drop her off at the door while you park the car.

Our good pastor friend, Louis Kayatin, provided an excellent example for me as a young husband by always opening the car door for his wife. If they ever went out and he forgot to open the car door, she would just simply stay seated in the car until he quickly returned and opened the door for her. Patti attempted to do that until I left her alone for a long time. Halfway through my meal I realized I had forgotten that Patti was still in the car. Just kidding! The only time that I would ever consistently open the door for Patti as a newly married man was when I knew that there were church people watching. Then I would go around and open the door for her. Needless to say, she was not happy with such behavior. At such times she did not view me as a gentleman but as a jerk! I really was being unkind because I was thinking of myself. I repented and quickly learned a gentleman serves his lady and is never a "show-off."

The older I get the more I realize that opening the door and assisting my wife is a way for me to show her how much I care for her. Another way that a husband can be a gentleman is in the way that he interacts with his wife in a crowd. When you are in a setting where your wife does not know anyone, it is very important that you stay with her and you introduce her to people and you include her in the conversation.

Patti and I attended my ten-year high school class reunion. Of course I knew everyone and she knew no one. I was like a social butterfly flittering and fluttering from one person to the next while my wife was completely lost in the crowd. The only person that she knew was my neighbor from across the street, Stuart. Stuart was kind enough to stay with her the whole night and keep her entertained. Boy was I a jerk! At the end of the evening, I was on a social high, having seen old friends and reliving the "good old days." Patti, on the other hand, was ready to wring my neck for abandoning her. Now when we are in a crowd of people that she doesn't know I purpose to stay with her, introduce her to new people, and include her in the conversation.

If we are in a crowd of people that we both know I still make eye contact with her. While involved in separate conversations I will periodically look at her, stare at her, wink at her, or even wave at her or blow her kisses. I want to let her know she is still important to me no matter where we are.

Gentlemen, one of the rudest things we can do is abuse our wife's time. For instance, when you tell her you are only going to be in the store for a minute and you come out twenty minutes later because you were talking to a friend that you met, she does not feel that you are treating her with respect and acting as a gentleman. Your word should be your bond and when you tell your wife that you are going to be a certain amount of time in a certain place, try your best to stay within those time parameters. When you know that you are going to be late from work, take the time to call your wife and explain to her why you are going to be late and approximately when you're going to be home and tell her how much you are looking forward to finally being reunited with her.

A gentleman is also patient and understanding with his wife when she is running late, even when she decides to change her clothes three times before she is ready to leave. For a man, clothing is a covering. For a woman, clothing is a feeling. She might look perfect in a certain dress, but she is not in the right mood to wear it. When she is finally ready, make sure to acknowledge the value that you place upon her taking the time to look her best. Do not make a big issue of the time involved. Obviously, a woman has more to do than a man does; she has to do her makeup, fix her hair, polish her fingernails, and coordinate accessories.

Getting the family ready to go to church used to be an incredible chore that added great stress to our marriage. I used to get myself ready quite quickly and go into the car in the garage and wait for Patti until the designated time to go, at which time I would begin to honk the horn. Needless to say, this did not help add harmony to our home or create marital bliss between us.

Today, Patti and I drive to church in two separate vehicles. We split up our large family by having me take the kids who are ready and the rest of them go later with Patti. Everyone is much happier. When she was growing up, Patti's father was much worse than I was about punctuality. As a teenager, Patti had great difficulty getting ready for church and so her dad would often honk the horn when she was not ready on time. So Patti decided she was going to really try and be ready on time one Sunday. She got herself up a little earlier, worked a little harder and she actually got ready on time for several weeks in a row without any honking by her dad. Her father decided that he enjoyed the honking so he decided to wake up earlier and reset the time to be ready by ten minutes earlier so that he could have the pleasure of honking at her once again.

Don't exasperate your wife! Do whatever you can to be able to make her life easier and to lift the pressure off her, not load the pressure on. A gentleman bears his wife's burdens instead of adding to them. The Holy Spirit is a perfect gentleman. He never will force Himself on us, coerce us, or manipulate us. He leads us and pulls us but doesn't push us. The Holy Spirit is a perfect example of a gentleman and when we all follow His example we can never go wrong. As we align ourselves with the work of the Holy Spirit in our relationship with our wives, it will cause us to grow spiritually and to have much happier, healthier marriages. Not only will it cause our earthly relationships to grow, but also our relationship with our Heavenly Father. As we honor our wives and treat them properly God says that our prayers will be unhindered and He promises to bless us with a closer relationship with Him too.

> ❧
> **DON'T EXASPERATE YOUR WIFE! DO WHATEVER YOU CAN TO BE ABLE TO MAKE HER LIFE EASIER.**

STICKING POINTS

❖ If your wife was asked if you are a gentleman, how would she respond?

❖ Are you a gentleman in private and/or in public?

❖ Begin to open your wife's car door this week, integrate a new "gentlemanly" activity, and remove a rude behavior (i.e., burping, et cetera).

Chapter Six

Pamper Your Wife

Honor one another above yourselves.

Romans 12:10 (NIV)

Most wives love to be pampered! Pampering your wife can take on many forms, including giving her a massage when she's tired or achy. You can get a bottle of scented massage oil for about fifteen dollars at the mall or online. It will last for months and make your wife feel like a queen.

Patti loves massages and we have even taken classes where we learned the proper massaging techniques. From time to time, I will send Patti to a professional masseuse, which she also enjoys immensely.

Pampering is indulging your wife's desires instead of your own. It may include watching a "chick flick" of her choice as you gently play with her hair, hold her hand, and cuddle closely. Be the runner for the beverages, popcorn, or whatever she wants to munch on while she relaxes.

ॐ

PAMPERING YOUR WIFE CAN TAKE ON MANY FORMS.

Going shopping with your wife may be the last thing you want to do, but it's an excellent way to pamper your wife. Don't complain, and instead, help her find that perfect outfit or item she is looking for.

Patti used to irritate me to no end when it came to shopping because we had a different viewpoint as to what shopping meant. To most men, shopping can be likened to a hunting experience. You see it, you shoot it, you bag it, and you bring it home. For most women, it's a visual learning experience. She wants to see "everything." Window shopping is fun to her as she learns about the latest fashions. She is in no hurry to buy anything until she has seen everything.

Patti would shop for hours and buy nothing and I would be ready to scream. I'd hand her things to buy and suggest to the clerks at stores that they tell her she looked great in certain clothes. I have learned great patience over the years as I have followed Patti around the malls of America. Be patient, let your wife take her time when she is shopping.

Another great way to pamper your wife is to fill her car up with gas, wash it, and vacuum it out. Most women don't really like to stand out in the driveway with a hose, wash their car, and apply the Blue Coral Car Wax. If you are short on time, have her car washed and waxed at a local car wash. When her car is not functioning properly, see to it that it gets fixed so that she is not left stranded and feels endangered.

Men, we expect our wives to help us but we need to go out of our way to help make their lives easier. When you are going out, ask her if you can get her anything at the store or run an errand for her. Don't wait for her to ask you, offer your errand-running services to her.

Pampering is not spoiling your wife but letting her know that she is number one in your life and the queen of your castle. We have five kids all still living at home so pampering Patti includes giving her a break from the kids, whether it be a ladies night out or by taking the kids bowling or somewhere else outside the house.

A great idea that I have not done yet is giving her a whole day off. It's called "Mom's Day Off." Give her a day where she does absolutely nothing around the house. She doesn't cook, clean, do yard work, or home-work with the kids. You and the kids do it all on "Mom's Day Off." I plan to try this very soon.

We need to learn to help each other. The Bible described Eve as a helpmate to Adam but I believe that a wise husband does a lot of helping himself!

STICKING POINTS

Operation Planned Pampering:

❖ Your mission, if you choose to accept it, is to look for every way to pamper your wife. Look for the small ways, not just the big ways that are easily noticeable.

❖ Since pampering is indulging in your wife's desires, make a list of ten things she likes and set a goal to do two or three of them each month throughout the year.

1._____

2._____

3._____

4._____

5._____

6._____

7._____

8._____

9._____

10._____

WOMEN
STICKING RELATIONALLY

CHAPTER SEVEN

Learn to Fight Fairly

Blessed are the peacemakers;
for they shall be called the children of God.

Matthew 5:9 (KJV)

My husband and I don't fight; we just have some "very intense fellowship" from time to time! Something we have both noticed over the years is that it takes me a lot longer to get over things than it does for him. It may be that my emotions are more involved in the reconciling process than his are. Let's face it, some men just don't want to deal with issues related to relationships. They would rather sweep things under the rug and pretend they aren't there until the bulge gets so big that everyone's tripping over it!

We need to deal with our hurts and hang-ups to the point that we give them a decent burial. Every married couple is going to have some big battles, and we need to learn how to fight fairly so that we won't bury each other. The number one rule for feuding with our husband is: don't get historical. Keep on the subject at hand; don't hit him below the belt with a reminder of one of his past failures.

Hewlett Packard had to downsize its Printed Circuit Board division and then reassign the workers. They held a New Orleans-style funeral, with all the flashy clothes and umbrellas and a jazz band. They marched through the plant and had the employees throw items that represented their lost jobs into a coffin. They then read a eulogy that was written about the now extinct division. Then in true New Orleans style, the jazz band changed the music from a dirge to a true Dixieland Jazz celebration. This gave closure to the displaced employees and their past victories and then a hope for the future successes to come.

We need to learn from history, not live there or be bound by it! When spouses get upset and emotions get churned up, logic can easily be overridden. It is okay to get angry and emotional. The Bible says it so well, "In your anger do not sin" (Ephesians 4:26 NIV). Deal with it! Tell him both what you feel and what you think. Let him respond to the issue at hand. Agree long before you go into the ring that you are not going to bring up past issues or you will inevitably create a break of trust. It takes lots of love and discipline to stay on track but it's worth it. You will become better problem solvers and minimize wounding one another's emotions if you don't get historical when you have a "marital moment."

The second rule of fighting fairly is, don't get hysterical! Sometimes we get so upset that we yell or talk so fast that we don't communicate anything but anger. Communication is a two-way street. We have to speak in such a manner that we are understood and actually have something meaningful to say. If, after you are done with your temper tantrum, your husband is left saying, "So, what's your point?" you are not communicating effectively. If you are ready to do him bodily harm with your bare hands, or worse yet with a weapon, you are not ready to talk. You are only ready to walk! Take a long walk until you are calm enough to make sense and hopefully be prepared to make reconciliation.

Sometimes I go to my bedroom, go for a walk, or just leave the room if I am too fired up to avoid saying things I would later regret. I need to collect my thoughts and subdue my emotions if I hope to be a peacemaker instead of a peace taker. Whatever you do, don't resort to cussing at one another. Recently a couple came to visit our church. They told me and my husband that they had some serious relationship problems and had come to the conclusion that they had to do two things to make things better. First, they said that they needed to start attending church, and second they had to stop cussing at one another when they fought. Just those two changes made a world of difference in their relationship. Another man who my husband knew well told him that the way he overcame his anger problem was by overcoming his cussing problem first. Regardless of what you think about cussing, it is totally out of bounds for any marriage!

> ℘ℭℜ
> ANGER MAY VERY WELL BE THE CANCER OF OUR SOULS AND NOT JUST OUR MARRIAGES.

Gary Smalley, a leading marriage counselor, author, and conference speaker says that anger is the number one enemy of marriages. The Bible states, "Do not let the sun go down while you are still angry" (Ephesians 4:26 NIV). Be quick to forgive your spouse and don't let anger simmer in your soul. Anger may very well be the cancer of our souls and not just our marriages. Forgiving someone privately in prayer with God and face-to-face with them alone is a powerful antidote to anger and will hasten the restoration of peace and harmony in your marriage and in your home!

STICKING POINTS

❖ What is the number one rule for feuding with your husband?

❖ What is the second rule of fighting fairly?

❖ List ways you can improve your response in "intense discussion," not just "intense fellowship" with your spouse.

_____

_____

_____

_____

_____

CHAPTER EIGHT

Don't Correct Him in Public

Excel in showing respect for each other.

Romans 12:10 (GWT)

A couple years ago my husband let me know in no uncertain terms how much he despised my correcting him in public! I didn't realize that he felt demeaned as a man and would rather be "taken out to the wood shed and beaten privately" than have me "slap his hands" in public. Ladies we all know men are not as concerned about the details of the story as we are. We may feel like a detail was missed or misrepresented but it is no big deal to them, and they don't want to be interrupted before or after the punch line.

One night we were out with a guest speaker and my husband told a story wrong. At that time I felt obligated to set the record straight. Instead, I set the "man on fire!" His disposition and attitude shifted suddenly, and I felt a very cool breeze blowing in my direction. My husband admitted he was wrong in the details but what I did devalued him. I did the right thing in the wrong way!

What Paul and many husbands want is simple! Praise him in public and correct him in private. Paul said, "Correct me as much as you need when we are alone but don't make me look bad when we are out with others!" This practice can save both of you from some embarrassing moments. Don't assume that you have the details correct yourself.

ॐ

PRAISE HIM IN PUBLIC AND CORRECT HIM IN PRIVATE.

What if you are wrong and when you correct him you end up getting corrected yourself? Worse yet, if you and he do not agree as to who is right about the disputed details you can go sixteen rounds together and both come out looking very beat-up.

Paul and I used to laugh at his now deceased grandparents that fought often over the "small stuff." Have you noticed how much older couples sweat the small stuff? When we fight as spouses it makes us both look bad and a lot older than we actually are! The place of agreement is the place of power and where there is a lack of agreement there will be a lack of power.

Allow your husband to make mistakes without telling him, "I told you so." We as wives know we don't want to hear that statement from our husbands, so apply the golden rule. Attitude is everything in a relationship. The Bible says, "Pride goes before destruction" (Proverbs 16:18 NIV). If your husband didn't listen to your words of wisdom and blew it, you don't have to remind him of his error. Let your track record speak for itself. When someone is already suffering due to a poor decision we are rubbing salt into their wounds if we nuke them with the "I told you so" line.

Marriage is a partnership and two heads are better than one. Let's be practical about this. If you criticize his poor decisions he will be much less likely to include you in future decision making and your influence will likely diminish in your household over time. Husbands want to be around wives who celebrate them not just criticize or tolerate them. What we respect rows towards us, what we disrespect rows away from us. See what good can possibly come of your husband's poor decisions and focus on that instead of the negative ramifications.

A wise wife does not expose her husband's weaknesses in public and is merciful towards him in private as well. "Blessed are the merciful, for they will be shown mercy" (Matthew 5:7 NIV).

What you sow will grow and come back to you like a boomerang. When we get married we become one flesh, so when we expose our spouse's weakness we are "exposing ourselves." People get arrested for indecent exposure every day! Don't go there! Build up your man publicly and privately, and he will see you as a contributor rather than a competitor in the market place of ideas!

STICKING POINTS

❖ What will agreement create in your marriage?

❖ How should you handle a conversation with your husband in the company of others when he is wrong with the details?

❖ List five ways you can verbally celebrate your husband.

1._____

2._____

3._____

4._____

5._____

CHAPTER NINE

Don't Nag

The tongue has the power of life and death,
and those who love it will eat its fruit.

Proverbs 18:21 (NIV)

One thing that many husbands complain about is a nagging wife! No woman wants to be labeled a nag. King Solomon in the Bible had seven hundred wives and three hundred concubines. He definitely had a woman problem. One of his reoccurring themes in Proverbs, the Book of Wisdom, is that of a nagging wife. Solomon writes, "A continual dripping in a very rainy day and a contentious woman are alike" (Proverbs 27:15 KJV).

Ladies, we don't need to always be talking. Turn off the flow of conversation from time to time. Don't be a drip, like a Chinese water torture. While men are often quick to point out the nagging fruits of a wife, they are often slow to discover the roots of the problem. Solomon had one thousand women that he was attempting to husband, all at the same time. Neglected wives can easily fall prey to the temptation to nag. Wives that have not been taken seriously or listened to are also great nagging candidates. All husbands should honor and respect their wives as equal partners in life. However, wives who have failed to forgive their husbands will also tend to sound like broken records at times.

Several years ago my husband was concerned about a man in the church whose wife came almost every Sunday but he rarely attended himself. She said her husband was very busy at work. He decided to call the man personally and find out what the problem was. Her husband explained an altogether different scenario to my husband. He admitted that he had committed adultery ten years ago and said that his wife reminded him every single day of his marital "mess up." He had problems with worshipping a God who would have his wife act in such a cruel manner.

When my husband discovered what was really happening, he called the wife on the carpet and told her that she can't say she has forgiven him and at the same time constantly remind him of his past failures. She confessed that she was wrong in her handling of her pain, and when she stopped the nagging he started coming to church and committed himself to the Lord. Nagging will not only drive a man away from his wife but can also drive him away from her faith if she is a believer.

Nagging, as defined by Webster, is "a persistent, critical, fault finding response that creates a sense of irritation in the one being nagged." Nobody wants to be around someone who irritates them! Ask your husband if he thinks you nag or irritate him in your daily conversations. Don't be defensive. Just listen.

Nags don't listen, they just keep talking and talking and talking, like the Energizer Bunny keeps going and going and going.

We have five children, two boys and three girls. Our middle daughter, Gabrielle, is appropriately nick-named "Gabby." We left her with Paul's parents for a few days and finally Paul's dad had reached his listening limit and said to her, "Gabby, I will give you a dime if you can just be quiet for one minute." She couldn't even shut her mouth for one minute even though she would have been paid to do so.

If you are listening to your husband instead of always talking, he will be much more likely to bare his soul and share his feelings with you. He will also be able to stay focused much better when you do speak if you take a break from talking and learn to listen to him. People who keep talking without taking a breath are just plain rude. I once was involved on a project with a woman who would not stop talking as soon as I got on the phone. She could talk for forty-five minutes straight without coming up for air. She may have thought she was being friendly but nothing could have been further from the truth. She was abusing other people's time and acting very selfishly.

> ଛଠଽ
> IF YOU ARE LISTENING TO YOUR HUSBAND INSTEAD OF ALWAYS TALKING HE WILL BE MUCH MORE LIKELY TO BARE HIS SOUL AND SHARE HIS FEELINGS WITH YOU.

Learn how to bury a conversation. Some conversations may please you but they are dead on arrival in regards to your husband. Give such conversations or subjects a decent burial and then don't dig up the bones! Some conversations will put you or your husband in an emotional comatose state and are better left unsaid as well.

When you speak make sure you are speaking words of life, not death. Words that encourage and build up lead to life. Words that discourage and tear down lead to death. When you see yourself going down the wrong road, make a U-turn. It is impossible to go the wrong direction and get to the right destination! The power of death and life are in the tongue and we must remember that nagging never leads to life.

STICKING POINTS

❖ Define the word "nagging."

❖ List three areas in your relationship with your husband that could cause you to nag.

1._____

2._____

3._____

❖ How can you correct the three things you listed above?

CHAPTER TEN

Romancing Romeo

Who is this young woman coming from
the wilderness with her arm around her beloved?

Song of Songs 8:5 (GWT)

My husband has been romantic with me since we began dating. The girls used to come to my dorm room and ask me to tell them about the romantic details of our dates. A few years ago he told me that he wanted me to be romantic too. I never thought he cared or needed to be romanced. As a younger man he was single dimensional and it was much simpler to please him. In midlife he wanted me to touch him emotionally and intimacy took on a much broader definition for him.

As men reach midlife they tend to become more balanced relationally with the woman in their life. Often men who have poured their lives into their careers at the expense of their marriages and families attempt to make up for lost time and unfortunately at times find their spouses and families have already "checked out" and found different relationships to emotionally bond with.

Romance for my husband met an emotional need that was either dormant or seemed to be nonexistent to me in the past. I have learned to "romance Romeo" and so can you!

One of the keys to romance is, always utilize the element of surprise. One day I surprised him by planting a very sexy lingerie item in his briefcase. When he got to work and opened his briefcase he immediately called me and shared his delight. I knew I had a responsibility to prepare myself to follow through with my romantic appeal that evening. If I had gotten too tired or had a headache that night it would have been a big let down for him and counterproductive.

> ∞CR
> ONE OF THE KEYS TO ROMANCE IS, ALWAYS UTILIZE THE ELEMENT OF SURPRISE.

I like to do big romantic birthday surprises. My desire is that when he closes his eyes to make a birthday wish that I can make his wishes and dreams come true. On his 40th birthday I took him to the Mall of America to shop at the world's biggest mall. Paul had a blast shopping and even riding on a roller coaster and other amusement park rides in this super mall.

On another birthday I surprised him with an overnight trip to a spa where we got a spa package, a delicious dinner, and a romantic room. More recently I blew his mind with an internet deal I lined up at a hotel at Niagara Falls. The balcony room overlooked the Horseshoe Falls and was a spectacular, romantic rendezvous for both of us.

I know a woman in our church that gave her husband hints leading him to a hotel room where she was waiting for him in the closet! He wasn't scared, he loved it! Ladies, we can be more romantic than we ever thought possible and add fuel to the romantic times in our marriages.

Besides birthdays, Valentine's Day, and Sweetest Day there are other ideal times to exercise your romantic gifting. My husband travels overseas almost every year for about two weeks. I want to let him know that he is loved, missed, and being thought about every single day. The way I romance him at such times will work wonders for any traveling spouse. I write him a card for every single day and I insert a very special romantic gift inside to make him look forward to his return home to me! The cards get hotter and hotter as the days go by. When he gets off the plane he is ready to run into my arms.

Just because many men suffer from RDD (Romantic Deficit Disorder) does not mean that we have to shut down our romantic abilities. Our creative surprise can create some healthy "romantic competition." No man likes to be outdone by his wife! You can "raise the romantic bar" with your well-timed romantic surprises at birthdays and throughout the entire calendar year.

STICKING POINTS

❖ How can you put romance back into your marriage?

❖ What is one big key to effective romance?

❖ Do one thing this week to raise the romantic bar in your relationship.

CHAPTER ELEVEN

Don't Replace Your Husband with the Kids

That they may teach the young women to be sober,
to love their husbands, to love their children.

Titus 2:4 (KJV)

There is a very common mistake that many new moms make after they start having children. The scenario unfolds something like this: An expectant couple cheerfully anticipates their new arrival by decorating the nursery, going to baby showers, telling all their friends the "good news," and taking Lamaze classes together to prepare.

The unsuspecting expectant couple is in for a big surprise. Little do they know that the last three months of pregnancy and the first three months following the birth are going to be some of the most stressful times of their marriage. Moms see their precious, helpless little babies and unconsciously make them the center of their universe.

I must admit, I actually went there with my kids. I love being a mom and with five children, it is more than a full-time job. It is so easy to feel that the needs of your tiny baby are more important than your husband's. Babies can't fend for themselves, but a husband should be self-sufficient.

I remember my husband telling me that he wanted more of my time and attention. I thought, "How selfish can you be?" Couldn't he see that I was nursing, nurturing a baby, and taking care of the house as well? By 4:00 PM each day I didn't think I could make it to dinner without falling asleep. My energy was gone and my body was worn out. As we had more and more children, they were constantly on top of me to the point where I could hardly even go to the bathroom alone. And yet, my husband wanted to be with me in the evenings while all I wanted was some peace and quiet.

One woman, on a recent TV talk show, was discussing her balancing act between her husband and children. She said that after having a child crawling on her all day the last thing she wanted was someone else crawling on her. She was referring to her husband's ongoing desire for sex. What is the answer to this huge dilemma that we moms must face?

I do not have all the answers but this I do know: one day the kids will be gone and you cannot neglect your relationship with your husband now and think you will have a happy, healthy relationship in the future. Put yourself in his place. How would you feel if your husband always gave his time and attention to the kids and put you on the back burner?

I have noticed over the years that whenever my husband took a new position at work, "I lost him" for many months. He would pour himself into his job, working seventy to ninety hours a week until he established some significant momentum. I must admit that his actions (if even just for a few months) caused me to feel emotionally neglected and I told him that I felt his job was "the other woman." Honestly, if he did

ഇയര

ONE DAY THE KIDS WILL BE GONE AND YOU CANNOT NEGLECT YOUR RELATIONSHIP WITH YOUR HUSBAND NOW AND THINK YOU WILL HAVE A HAPPY, HEALTHY RELATIONSHIP IN THE FUTURE.

not put our relationship back into balance, our marriage would have become a mess.

We had to talk about it. You cannot correct what you do not confront! We talked for hours until we came back into balance. Balance is a key in life. Talking and communicating helped us come to a better under-standing of one another's needs and how we might meet them.

We came to realize that our marriage relationship always needs to be the priority relationship, even though there might be some big-time interruptions, i.e., new baby, moving eight times in ten years, starting new jobs, multimillion-dollar building programs, building a new home, et cetera. Kids need to see two parents loving each other and the children as well. One of the greatest ways you can love your children is to love their dad and let them see a well-balanced, healthy marriage modeled before them.

Our kids do not set the atmosphere in our home. We, as parents, filter the attitudes and actions of the children; we do not cater to their every wish and whim. We had to learn that spoiling a child is not an act of love but an act of neglect. We need to help our children grow up and assume responsibility, not become dependent on us for the rest of their lives. By constantly prioritizing children over our spouse, we diminish their views of marriage and contribute to their living a self-centered life. When husbands take the third, fourth, or fifth place in the home it won't be long until our homes are "out of order."

Many marriages fail after the last child leaves the home. We learned that to have a strong marriage that would outlast the child rearing years some new courses of action had to be taken. We took steps almost seven years ago and implemented a weekly date night. We spend quality, one-on-one time together doing things we both like to do. The focus of these nights is us, not the kids, work, or anyone else. It worked so well that we decided to take a one week vacation each year alone, just the two of us. Wow! It has been such a marriage regenerator! If you cannot get away for a week, try to go for at least a weekend.

> ဆာ
> BY CONSTANTLY PRIORITIZING CHILDREN OVER OUR SPOUSE, WE DIMINISH THEIR VIEWS OF MARRIAGE AND CONTRIBUTE TO THEIR LIVING A SELF-CENTERED LIFE.

Parents, we need to stick together if we are going to stay together. As hard as our kids have tried to manipulate and divide us with their individual agendas, we have stood our ground. Paul will not allow the kids to sass me or demean me and tells them, "Don't talk to my wife like that!" He lets them know that I am his wife before I am their mother and I stand up for him in front of the kids as well. Whatever you do, don't fall into the "parent trap" of putting your kids always in front of your husband, unless you want him to leave when they do!

STICKING POINTS

❖ What is one of the greatest ways you can love your children?

❖ Do you need to bring balance back into your home?

❖ Set a date night for you and your husband and don't talk about anything but each other.

MEN
STICKING PRACTICALLY

Chapter Twelve

Be Her Superhero

A friend loves at all times.

Proverbs 17:17 (NIV)

My youngest son, Gideon, thinks he is a superhero. Every day he dresses up in a different superhero costume. Some days he is Batman, others he is Spiderman, or sometimes even Superman. He is always eager to fight the evil villains on behalf of his mother as he runs around the house in his cape holding various weaponry. You can be your wife's superhero and be a super husband on her bad days.

Everyone from time to time has a bad day. It may be a "bad hair" day, a "bad boss" day, a "bad kids" day, or bad "time of the month" day. It may not be a national crisis to you if she had a flat tire and is late to get the kids to school, but nevertheless, it means a lot to her if you make some effort to soften the blow for her.

Here are six sensational things you can do to come to the rescue and be her superhero:

1. Take her, or even the whole family, out to dinner if she has had a particularly rough day. This is a

chance for her to enjoy a meal without having the responsibility of cooking it, serving it, and cleaning up afterwards. Leave the burnt roast on the stove. Leave the toys on the floor and give her a break from having to cook. Women are much more into food than men are. When men go out to eat, they are finished in thirty minutes. With women, it is two hours. If you ask a man what he had to eat, he says, "steak." The woman describes every item on the plate, how each one tasted, the dessert, the color of the tablecloth and plates. For men it is a meal, but for women it is much more.

2. Take the kids out for a field trip or just out of the house. With five children, Patti very rarely is home alone! Taking the kids to the park, hiking, biking, or going to see a movie are some of the best things you can do to help your wife relieve tension and stress. Make sure the kids have fun so that when they come back they aren't complaining to Mom.

3. Take her out yourself and leave the kids at home. Of course if the children are little you will need an adult family member or babysitter to stay with the children. Take her to her favorite restaurant, the park, or the mall if you have some money to burn. Shopping works for Patti, but it can create a habit that is very expensive and can generate some bad days for you if you overuse this one. It is not about money, it is about time spent together, supporting her emotionally, and letting her know you are her superhero.

4. Be sensitive towards her at her time of the month. I have often said PMS means "punish my spouse,"

but if you treat her extra special she may reward you rather than punish you. Find out what she needs during those "difficult days." Some women crave chocolate or another certain food, others just want to be left alone. During this time, do not forget that she may say or do things that she normally wouldn't. Be understanding and sensitive to the fact that she is not feeling like herself so she might not act like herself. Give her a break and some space and when it is all over she will remember the times you came to her rescue.

5. Listen to her. When your wife has had a trouble-filled day she does not want you to tell her how she could have avoided it or how she can fix it. She wants you to listen to what she experienced and how she felt. When she wants your thoughts or solutions, she will let you know. Hug her while you listen without grabbing or groping her. You might want to physically bond on your bad day but for her, she wants to emotionally bond with you. A superhero might not always be there all the time, but they always come to the rescue in a time of crisis and "save the day."

> &)CR
> SHE WANTS YOU TO LISTEN TO WHAT SHE EXPERIENCED AND HOW SHE FELT.

6. Help her out when company is over! One of the most stressful times for a woman is when she is entertaining. She wants everything to look right and work right. Many women feel like they are going to the Olympics and the guests are either going to give them a gold, silver, bronze, or no

medal at all. They feel that the house is more of a reflection of them then of us. Help her with cleaning things you would never clean, buying things you would never buy, and doing things you would never do to make the house look and even smell it's best for "showtime."

STICKING POINTS

❖ Do you believe you can be your wife's super-hero?

❖ Of the five superhero suggestions, which three will you do to rescue her this month?

1._____

2._____

3._____

CHAPTER THIRTEEN

Help Around the House

Two are better than one, because they have a good return for their work: if one falls down, his friend can help him up. But pity the man who falls and has no one to help him up!

Ecclesiastes 4:9-10 (NIV)

There are some women of a certain tribe in Africa that perform an unusual "balancing act." Once a year they balance on their heads a big basket containing either their husband or their sweetheart. Unfortunately there are some women even in the 21st century who perform another extremely difficult balancing act of working outside of the home and solely managing the house as well.

Husbands, even if you work sixty hours a week and your wife is a full-time homemaker, you will be wise to help out around the house. Remember, your wife is your lover, not your mama! A husband is to be a servant leader, someone who leads by example, not

> ෨෬
>
> A HUSBAND IS TO BE A SERVANT LEADER, SOMEONE WHO LEADS BY EXAMPLE, NOT BY GIVING COMMANDS.

by giving commands. A surefire way to show you care about your wife is to voluntarily help with household duties.

I heard about a couple who would wake up together early in the morning and they both liked to drink coffee. The problem was, neither one of them wanted to make the coffee so they often argued as to who was going to make the coffee from day to day. Well, one day they got in another one of their big coffee making arguments and finally the exasperated wife asked her husband a question. "If I can show you in the Bible that men are to make the coffee, will you make the coffee from now on?" He thought about it for a minute and said, "Sure, show it to me in the Bible." With a big smile she said, "He-brews."

Don't make your wife outsmart you to get you to provide her with a little assistance around the house. Start by picking up your own dirty socks and under-wear. It is not your wife's job to pick up after you! If you have a problem getting motivated, put a basket-ball hoop on your clothes hamper.

My wife recently noticed that our teenage son, Jordan, wasn't rinsing his plate after he ate and she told him, "One day you will be living on your own and you won't have me around cleaning up after you. You need to learn how to do it yourself." He informed his mother that he was not concerned about getting prac-tice for the future because, "When I leave here I'm getting married and my wife will take care of it." Patti almost executed him on the spot and he got a speech from both of his parents.

Dads, not only do you need to help around the house, but you also need to be the primary motivator of your children to assist in their household duties. Often Patti sends me upstairs to inspect the children's rooms to insure that they have straightened up.

Men, doing household chores doesn't mean that you have to put on an apron and become "Suzy Homemaker," but it does mean that you take responsibility for dividing up household duties both inside and outside the house. Divide the household tasks by skill sets and your individual desires.

About ten years ago I got excited because I noticed more and more women mowing their lawns. I pointed out those liberated neighborhood ladies to Patti and suggested that she start mowing the lawn. She told me about how as a teenager she ran the lawnmower into the side of her parent's house and left a hole in it. Needless to say, Patti does not have to mow the lawn, but she does do most of the cooking and the laundry. I do a lot of general household cleaning, all the book-keeping, and the household maintenance. I keep the cars washed and running well, paint, help with the decorating of the house, and even take out the trash.

Things really get good when I slip over to Patti's side of the household task list and help her cook and clean up after dinner. Seeing her man work around the house is a big turnon for many wives and it will definitely demonstrate you care.

Fix things around the house that are broken. I actually know a man who holds the ladder for his wife to climb up on the roof to do the repair work. It is amazing that they are still married. I guess she does not know that husbands normally do such dangerous jobs. If you are not a handyman, hire someone. Do not make her try to fix things around the house.

Just the other day, Patti almost had to plunge the toilet for the first time. I couldn't get to it so our son, Jordan, came to the rescue. Patti doesn't get into toilet plunging so I make it my job. And while we are on the subject of toilets, lift the toilet seat and then return it back to its proper lowered position.

Husbands, if you want to better your relationship with your wife, sit down and talk to her about the division of household labor and ask her how you can help make her load lighter and her life easier.

STICKING POINTS

* Do you lead by example by helping out around the house?

* This week ask your wife what you can do to help her around the house.

* Honestly, have you seen a need and thought, "Oh, my wife will do that or pick it up?"

* Next time, see the need and take care of it. This week do something around the house without being asked.

CHAPTER FOURTEEN

Gift Giving

Many curry favor with a ruler,
and everyone is the friend of a man who gives gifts.

Proverbs 19:6 (NIV)

Gifts help us to express the depth of our love and relationship. Gifts are also symbolic of the way that we feel toward our wife or the one we may be dating.

Dr. Gary Chapman, author of *The Five Love Languages* explains, "people express and receive love primarily in five different ways . . ."

1. Quality Time
2. Words of Affirmation
3. Acts of Service
4. Physical Touch
5. Gift Giving

Even though her primary love language may not be gift giving, every wife appreciates it when her husband gives her gifts. Dr. Gary Chapman makes an excellent observation in his chapter on "Receiving Gifts" where he says, "I examined the cultural patterns surrounding love and marriage and found that in every culture I studied, gift giving was a part of the love-marriage process." Gift giving transcends cultural barriers and is an excellent way to express love.

When I started dating Patti over twenty-five years ago, it didn't take me long to begin the gift-giving process. Soon after we began dating, Patti told me that her pillow was worn out. I went to the store and bought her a wonderful, fresh pillow. I told her as I gave it to her that I wanted her to think and dream about me as she laid her head on it. She cherished that pillow for years. It was a simple gift, but it showed that I cared about her and her personal needs. *Give a gift that shows you care.*

> ℘ℭ℞
> EVERY WIFE APPRECIATES IT WHEN HER HUSBAND GIVES HER GIFTS.

Soon after, I gave her a music box. I put in it a poem I had written that was straight from my heart to hers. The tune, *You Light up My Life,* was played on that music box and she still has it to this very day. *Make sure that the gift you give is something she actually wants.*

I also had told Patti that I wanted to give her flowers and it would be a symbol of our relationship. I started by giving her one single rose. When I gave her the rose, I told her the rose symbolized to me that she was my friend. Then I gave her three roses which symbolized that she was not just a friend, but a very special friend. Later, I gave her five roses symbolizing that I liked her very much. Next, I gave her seven roses to symbolize that I was in love with her and that this was true love. Finally, the night that I proposed to Patti, I gave her twelve roses symbolizing that I wanted her to be my wife for life. She was totally enthralled with each of the rose gifts that I gave to her. She highly anticipated the twelfth rose as, throughout this process, I had always told her about the next rose coming up. It really meant something between us and was, and still is, a symbol of our relationship. Now that I have been married to Patti for over twenty years, I still continue to give her flowers, as well as a wide assortment of other gifts. I realize the value that Patti places on receiving gifts; so I demonstrate how much I value her as my forever friend and lover through special gifts. *Give gifts that show you value her.*

Gifts do not have to be expensive and they do not have to be the traditional gifts of flowers, cards, and candy. Consider things that just show you are thinking of her. For instance, come home one day with her favorite dessert. When she is least expecting it, call her up sometime during the day and tell her that you are thinking about her and that you can't get her off your mind. Or give her a gift certificate to a favorite boutique, spa, or restaurant.

Gifts do not need to cost a lot of money; in fact, they might not cost any money at all. It might be giving her the gift of some time, when she knows that you are very busy but still make time to be with her, talk to her, and to share your lives together. It means more than any trinket you could buy. You might make a card or write some things on personal stationary that express your love for her. Give her some "Love Coupons." Years ago, I gave Patti a book of "Love Coupons" that I had personally designed. There were things like, "One Immediate Phone Hang Up," when I'm on the phone and not paying enough attention to you. "One Weekend Getaway to the Place of Your Choice." "A Seven Minute Hug." I gave those "Love Coupons" to her over fifteen years ago and she still has them, waiting for a new set. She was so impressed with the thought that she hasn't even used all of them yet! *Gifts don't have to be expensive.*

One year after we were married I decided to give Patti a special, personalized license plate which read, "#1 Beauty." Patti was pregnant at the time and was feeling anything but beautiful. I had no idea how much attention this personalized plate would actually get. Patti got tired of being stared at so she begged me to take this license plate off. I thought she was being ungrateful until one day when I was driving her car. I was at a stoplight and I had three guys staring and smiling at me while I was waiting for the light! That is the day I decided to get rid of the "#1 Beauty" license plate. *Give gifts that are going to be appreciated by the recipient.*

Pay attention husbands! Make sure that you are listening closely to what your wife says, because she is often dropping hints as to what she would like you to get for her. Many of us have absolutely no clue when our wives give us their signals. For instance, you and your wife may be shopping, looking at a sweater, and she says, "Boy, I'd like to have a sweater like that some day." What she is saying is that she would like to have that sweater very soon, not when she is ready to retire. My wife's personal line is, "I've always wanted one of those." When she says that, the lights and sirens go off and I immediately make a mental note. Men are much less subtle when they want something. They just simply say, "I want that!" Women use the power of suggestion. You must learn to speak her language and think like she thinks, and you will become richly rewarded.

The reality is even women admit that they don't know what they want because they so often change their mind. Their feelings and emotions can change quickly too, like the direction of the wind. A smart husband is like a good sailor, making adjustments and going with the flow. Sometimes you just have to ask your wife straight up, "What is it that you would like?" But don't do it the day before her birthday or anniversary or Christmas. Ask her far enough in advance and at an inconspicuous time so that she doesn't know you are trying to get clues for an upcoming special occasion. Your wife can tell the amount of time and effort you spent in obtaining the gift you are giving.

Believe it or not, the effort is just as important as the expense involved for the gift you give. Some gifts will take you much time and effort to search for. *Your wife will greatly appreciate all the extra effort you take in finding the perfect gift.*

One of the gift-giving mistakes that some men make is they attempt to give gifts that are supposed to last for years. For instance, they might give their wife an expensive ring and say, "This is for the next three birthdays, Christmases, and Anniversaries." No matter how nice the ring is, such a strategy is a big mistake. A big gift should be given from time to time as your funds permit, but never one gift for multiple occasions.

As a young husband, I thought it would be best to pace myself in the way that I gave gifts to Patti. Thinking that somehow I would spoil her if I did, I never gave her any extravagant gifts. Now as I have entered into midlife, I realize that giving extravagant gifts is an awesome opportunity for me to lavish my love upon her. Solomon was one of the wisest men who ever walked the earth, and he was generous in gift giving. After twenty plus years of marriage, I have come to the conclusion that Patti has given so much to me that there is no gift too large or too valuable that I could ever give her. Do not be afraid to spoil your wife! First of all, she probably deserves it, and secondly, never forget that you are one with her. When you are generous with your wife, you are being generous with yourself.

> ☙❧
>
> A BIG GIFT SHOULD BE GIVEN FROM TIME TO TIME AS YOUR FUNDS PERMIT, BUT NEVER ONE GIFT FOR MULTIPLE OCCASIONS.

One of the worst things a husband can do is to completely forget his wife's birthday or their wedding anniversary. Mark these dates in your day-planning calendar and make sure that you are ready, far in advance, with the right gift. Quality, handmade gifts can go a long way. Low quality, handmade gifts could get you in the doghouse. If you are a great carpenter, make her that hutch or the entertainment center she wants. Something you made for her that was close to professional quality would really be a source of pride for both of you, and less expensive than if you bought it. If you are not a great carpenter, you would be better off buying it for her. Whatever you do, don't forget to give gifts on special occasions. However, gifts are sure to be appreciated anytime. Be spontaneous, be creative, and be generous with whatever resources God has blessed you with.

Soon after we were married, Patti had a birthday and I decided to give her some gifts. I bought her a badminton set, a croquet set, and a toaster. When Patti opened her three gifts, she was totally underwhelmed. She almost wrapped the badminton set around my head, and expressed to me in no uncertain words that she did not enjoy the gifts I was giving her, especially since I was the one who loved badminton and croquet. She explained to me that when it came time to give her gifts, I should give her gifts that make her feel special and unique as a woman, not gifts that I would want for myself. Honestly, because I like practical gifts, I would have been very happy with the trio of gifts that I presented to Patti! Give her gifts that make her feel special and unique as a woman.

STICKING POINTS

❖ Has your wife dropped hints of things she would like to have?

❖ Would you rate yourself a good gift giver?

❖ Of the five love languages, how does your wife express and receive love?

❖ Of the five love languages, how do you express and receive love?

❖ Plan on giving your wife a gift you know she would love and give it to her when she least expects it.

CHAPTER FIFTEEN

The Ultimate Act of Love

For, brethren, ye have been called unto liberty;
only use not liberty for an occasion to the flesh,
but by love serve one another.

Galatians 5:13 (KJV)

Do you have a control issue? If you do, it could likely show up when you are watching television. Many men show more love and attention to their TV sets than to their wives. The one and only time that Patti was ever spanked by her father was when she walked in front of his TV set. Most husbands won't attempt to spank their wives for getting in front of the TV, but they will oftentimes throw a temper tantrum if their wife takes the remote and starts to change the channel.

Only God knows how many marriages have been upended by a little electronic device. Men can be very motivated by something as simple as a remote control. I heard of one wife who couldn't get her husband motivated to do his sit-ups until she put the remote control in between his toes. The average home in America has 2.24 TV sets, making it unnecessary for many spouses to watch TV together. Watching TV or movies may not be the best use of time but it is time together nevertheless. The next suggestion may be the ultimate act of sacrifice for a man. Give her the remote control one night and let her watch whatever she wants. When a man gives up his remote control, his wife knows it is true love. The way to exasperate her is to take the remote from her while she is watching an emotional movie and change the channel to the ball game. Look out!

Let's face it. Men and women oftentimes don't want to watch the same shows. You may prefer to watch a three-hour football game while she wants to see a "chick flick." Be a "good sport" and as long as you are not missing the Super Bowl, World Series, NBA Finals, or some other ultraimportant sporting event, let her watch whatever she wants.

My wife doesn't enjoy watching sports on TV. She says I could save a lot of time by just watching CNN Headline News to see the scores scroll at the bottom of the screen. Guys, we all know that's not much fun. Sometimes my wife will watch sports to please me and sometimes I will watch her movie or show to let her know that I want to be with her and make her happy.

I cannot believe I am confessing this, but it is true. As I have gotten older and entered into my second decade of marriage, I have found myself actually enjoying some "chick flicks" with my wife. Letting her watch what she wants is a great opportunity for the two of you to further bond together and to show her you really care about her feelings and emotions.

While you are watching her show, why not ask her if she would like a pop and some popcorn? Serve her! Wait on her hand and foot! We have some friends who like to stay up and watch Jay Leno while they give each other foot massages. You can do a lot of nice things for her while watching her show. When you follow the Bible's principles you will learn that it is your job to out-serve your wife, not outsmart her by means of attempting to control her.

My wife, Patti, has reminded me many times that I am not her boss. Unfortunately, in too many marriages power struggles change small issues like "who gets the remote control" into big issues. We need to serve one another in love. It would be great if the only thing men tried to control was the remote control! I have seen many men run their marriages into the ground by trying to control their wives. We can do this by belittling our spouse, telling them what they can and cannot do, and by just being bossy. Wives want to have a husband, not a boss, private investigator, or a judge.

> **ଛୁଠେଷ**
> **WHEN YOU FOLLOW THE BIBLE'S PRINCIPLES YOU WILL LEARN THAT IT IS YOUR JOB TO OUT-SERVE YOUR WIFE, NOT OUTSMART HER BY MEANS OF ATTEMPTING TO CONTROL HER.**

Are you smothering her with interrogating questions, critical comments, or consistently infringing on your wife's personal time and space? If so, it's time to realize two things. You are not God Junior and God the Father needs to be the one in control of both of you!

Too many husbands have remote control attitudes and actions that actually turn their wives off rather than on. Giving God control of your wife and your life is always a good decision!

Sticking Points

❖ Are you in a power struggle with your wife?

❖ Find two ways to out-serve your wife and put them into practice!

1._____

2._____

Chapter Sixteen

Bedroom Etiquette

For He gives to His beloved even in his sleep.

Psalm 127:2 (NASB)

Let's face it; we spend a lot of time in bed. Nearly one-third of your life you are in bed and if you are an average couple you will spend more time together in bed than together outside of bed. Sorry guys, I'm referring to sleep right now and not sex. I was counseling with a couple who were experiencing intimacy issues and one of the first things I asked them was whether they were going to bed at the same time. It turned out that she had to wake up early and he didn't, so he stayed up late working. They were not meeting each others' sexual needs. I got him to change his extra work hours from late at night to the early morning and things are heating up again. The number one *taboo* for couples is to go to bed at different times.

The number two *taboo*: Letting anyone sleep in your bed other than your spouse. We have five kids and we have had two dogs, but we do not let them in our bed. Children sleeping in your bed will not only wreck whatever romantic possibilities exist but they will steal precious sleep from your life.

Patti used to allow Promise to sneak in the bed on her side when she was a toddler. That all stopped when she started kicking Patti like a bucking bronco. If kids have nightmares they can either sleep on the floor next to your bed or be escorted back to their rooms. We keep a blanket under the bed and an extra pillow on hand for such occasions.

The number three *taboo*: Casting aside your manners at bed time. It is not fair for one spouse to take both sides of the bed or to steal the covers. Living in cold Cleveland, Ohio for our entire marriage we have learned how important it is for both of us to stay warm. I must confess I used to be a blanket bandit. I would wrap myself up in the covers like a cocoon and find Patti's uncovered frozen body in the morning. Needless to say she was not a happy camper. I learned to just lay the covers over my body instead of wrapping the covers underneath by body and doing my mummy routine in bed every night.

Another bad habit I had was waking up early in the morning and turning on the lights and slamming doors. I stopped when Patti threatened to give me a taste of my own medicine. Other in bed no-no's include eating food, picking your nose, or farting under the sheets. If you snore do whatever you can to get help from a doctor or specialist. Earplugs some-times work in light snoring cases.

The number one bedtime marriage *builder* is spending time talking together before you go to sleep. This may be the most private time of the day where you can talk about anything and everything that is on your mind. I like to talk about the day's highlights and my plans for the next. Patti likes to fill me in with the details of her day and what is going on in our five children's lives.

The number two bedtime marriage *builder* is to have her lay her head on your chest so you can massage her neck and back or play with her hair. There may be no better time to caress and love on one another than when you are lying in bed. A hand massage is a very relaxing way to end a day and it doesn't have to take away from your talk time. Nonsexual, affectionate touching is definitely the way to start to unwind and if your wife is interested in more than that she will let you know.

The number three bedtime marriage *builder* is to pray together before you go to sleep. You will become intimate with those you pray with and pray for. Since the husband is called of God to be the spiritual leader of the house, you should be the one to initiate prayer for your wife and family. We pray for each other, ask the Lord to guard our dreams from any evil influences and He does. Prayer keeps us close to each other and to God so that we can sleep in peace and rise up the next day rested and ready to tackle the tasks before us.

> ෨෬
>
> YOU WILL BECOME INTIMATE WITH THOSE YOU PRAY WITH AND PRAY FOR.

What happens at bedtime will not only affect your sex life but your whole life. Follow these simple bedtime instructions and you will make bedtime one of the best times of your entire day.

STICKING POINTS

❖ What bedroom etiquette habits do you need to improve upon?

❖ Pray together with your wife before going to bed.

Women
STICKING PRACTICALLY

CHAPTER SEVENTEEN

Give Him a She-Mote Control

Be good friends who love deeply;
practice playing second fiddle.

Romans 12:10 (The Message)

I heard a story of a woman who was checking out at a retail store. As she fumbled through her purse to pay for what she was purchasing, the clerk noticed a remote control for a TV in her purse. "So, do you always carry your TV remote?" the clerk asked. "No," she replied, "but my husband refused to come shopping with me, so I figured this was the best way to pay him back." Marriage is not about paybacks, getting revenge, or seeing how much you can get out of your spouse. It's about making deposits and giving your best to your mate!

We all know how much men love remote controls; how about giving him a "she-mote" for a day or two! A "she-mote" is letting your husband push the button that he wants as you aim to please him! Everyone has heard of the golden rule. "Do unto others as you would have them do unto you." The platinum rule is, "Love others in the ways and means by which they want to be loved."

The first thing you can do is make a sincere attempt to get in his world. What does your husband love to do? Fishing, golfing, bowling, skiing; these things may be the last things, you want to do, but if he loves to do these things, you are showing him great love if you will attempt to try something new! Whatever you do, don't complain about it if you are bold enough to venture out of your box of familiar experiences. You might not think you enjoy hiking or biking but think about it, when you were dating you were willing to do or try just about anything as long as you could be with your man!

When dating Paul, I went on off-road dirt bike trails, long hikes, and was even willing to push start his broken down car to be with him. Let's face it ladies, many times after marriage we go our separate ways and then wonder what ever happened to the romance, caring, and sharing. It's tough to share your life together when you don't spend any time together because you only focus on your personal pleasures in life! Start living the platinum rule today by asking your husband what he would love doing with you other than sex and see what he says! Unless it is illegal or immoral give it a shot and you may find a new and improved shopping friend!

The "she-mote" control doesn't end with your husband deciding what he wants to do but also where he would like to go. Maybe he has a favorite place to eat or hang out that really rocks his boat. My husband loves Dave and Busters and has his favorite video game, the Daytona Race Cars. He loves it when I agree to go and race the Daytona Race Cars but he hates it when I win. Believe it or not, husbands have a wish list of what they would like their wives to do. Many men say they want women who do activities with them. The days of "guy things" and "girl things" are fading fast! Girls can kickbox, wrestle, and play football now! I'm not going that far but most of us could stretch a little more in venturing out in regards to activities our husbands like to do. Attitude is everything! If you aren't good at first, don't get mad at him or yourself. Keep on trying until you can say you gave it your best shot. If you learn to laugh at yourself in the process you and your husband will enjoy the ride much, much more!

One of the best ways to dig out of a marital rut is to try something new together. I never liked to dance. I feel like everybody's watching me and I don't have much rhythm. In high school and in college my husband danced and loved it! He has begged me for years to dance with him at weddings and other special occasions. I repeatedly turned him down unless we were slow dancing with a bunch of old people we didn't know. Well recently, he nearly begged me to take swing dancing lessons with him. I actually picked it up faster than he did and we had a blast doing something new together. When you do something your husband loves to do, and gladly join him in going out to his kind of places from time to time, it is better than giving him the remote control. When you give him that "she-mote" control it helps you rekindle your love life.

> ℘∝
> ONE OF THE BEST WAYS TO DIG OUT OF A MARITAL RUT IS TO TRY SOMETHING NEW TOGETHER.

Sticking Points

❖ What is one of the best ways to dig out of a marital rut?

❖ What ways can you stretch a little and venture out to try new activities with your husband?

❖ When was the last time you made a deposit in your spouse's account? Try making one this week!

CHAPTER EIGHTEEN

Home "Reentry"

She looks well to how things go in her household.

Proverbs 31:27 (AMP)

One of the most dangerous segments on a manned NASA Space Mission is the reentry from outer space into the Earth's atmosphere. Upon reentering the atmosphere on February 1, 2003, the Columbia orbiter suffered a catastrophic failure due to a breach that occurred during launch when falling foam from the external tank struck the reinforced carbon panels on the underside of the left wing. The orbiter and its seven crew members were lost approximately fifteen minutes before the Columbia was scheduled to touch down at Kennedy Space Center.

Reentry into the love atmosphere can also be very dangerous to the success of your marriage mission. Like a spacecraft needs a heat shield to survive the transition, so too you can be such a heat shield to your husband when he returns home from work! The space-craft must enter the Earth's atmosphere at a precise angle or it will risk being set on fire, crash, and burn.

This chapter will give you some new angles that you can use in your home for happy, safe landings to come!

Husbands never want to come home to chaos! If the kids have trashed the house it is important to clean up and clear out the toys and "kid stuff" before he arrives! The house does not need to be

ఴౠ

HUSBANDS NEVER WANT TO COME HOME TO CHAOS!

spotless but there does need to be at least a path for him to get inside without breaking his neck. When Paul walks into our house I give him time and space in order to decompress. After ten minutes he has time to change clothes, read the mail, or possibly check his voice-mail messages.

Every man has his own after work rituals and some take longer than others. One lady in our church told us that when she sees her husband in his shorts after work that he is ready to talk and deal with whatever she's got. What is important is that you do not drop a bomb on him when he comes home, i.e., broken washing machine, big unpaid bill, kid flunking out of school, leaky roof, you wrecked the car, et cetera. No man wants to come home to a war zone. This is not a time for emotional confrontations. Shield him from crying, fussy kids! You may have held a crying baby all day and be totally worn out but that doesn't mean as soon as he puts down the briefcase you hand him a whiny child. Just give him a little time and he will come to the rescue with a much better attitude.

Wives, we can set the tone in our homes by having the right kind of attitudes when our husbands come home!

Philippians 2:5 (GWT) in the Bible says, "Have the same attitude that Christ Jesus had." What kind of attitude did Jesus have?

1. He had a selfless attitude (Philippians 2: 3-4).
2. He had a secure attitude (Philippians 2: 6-7).

Insecure wives attack their husbands when they walk in the door with their list of unsolved family and personal stories, but secure wives know that Rome wasn't built in a day and it will take time and mutual effort to solve most family issues!

You may want to give him a quick kiss and hug, a brief "I love you," but don't require it if he doesn't want any affection at this time. What you are doing is creating good memories in his mind of what it is like to come home. It is not a good idea to have unexpected company over often as a man wants his home to be his refuge! The more peaceful and "hassle free" your home environment is the more he will want to get home and stay home.

If you are in a dual-income home you may be coming home to a husband, a babysitter, an empty house, et cetera. The same principles apply regardless of who gets home first. A good first impression sets the pace for the rest of your day. You can only make one first impres-

&)cર

MAKE YOUR FIRST IMPRESSION ON HIM YOUR BEST IMPRESSION!

sion upon one another at the end of your work day so do your best to give your spouse their "unwinding time" or personal space. Keep initial conversations positive and put on your happy face. Show excitement in seeing your man and being reunited after a long day away! Make your first impression on him your best impression! Don't look like you just crawled out of bed when you first see him. When we look good we feel good about ourselves and others (including our spouses) will pick up our positive sentiments.

Make the atmosphere of your home attractive and a happy place to come home to. One of the definitions Webster's dictionary uses for atmosphere is "a work of art." Ask yourself, what picture am I painting on the canvas of my husband's mind of myself and our home? Artwork in a home or office often makes a great or poor first impression. Let the domino effect work in your favor when you make a great first impression after work or after being away from one another!

STICKING POINTS

❖ How can you set the tone in your house better for your husband's arrival from work?

❖ List two attitudes that Jesus had as listed in the book of Philippians, chapter two.

1._____

2._____

❖ How can you make your "first impression" more positive?

CHAPTER NINETEEN

Learn the Art of Timing

*The right word at the right time
is like a custom-made piece of jewelry.*

Proverbs 25:11 (The Message)

The Bible says in Ecclesiastes 3:1 (NIV) that "there is a time for everything." Timing really is everything both in relationships and in life. There is a time to ask for favors or help, and a time to be silent. In the Bible, Queen Esther is a great example of a wife who understood such timing. She prepared herself before she approached the king requesting a big favor. First of all, she prepared a great meal for him and a specially chosen guest (Esther 5:4). Esther fasted and prayed about what she was going to ask her husband for.

She dressed herself up so that she would look her best (Esther 5:1) and even smelled her best. This young wife also set the atmosphere of the banquet to be so pleasing to her husband that he asked her, "What is your request? Even up to half the kingdom, it will be given you" (Esther 5:3 NIV). Esther's request was granted her because she understood the art of timing and setting the right atmosphere.

Atmosphere is everything! When things are chaotic, messy, or noisy around the house don't push the envelope by sharing your lifetime wish list with your husband. A common request for many wives is asking their husbands to fix things around the house. Let's face it, a truly motivated handyman is hard to find. The honey-do lists we write out from time to time should not be like a ransom note or a grocery shopping list. It is not only what you say but how you say it that sets the atmosphere in your house.

For instance, if you tell him it better be done by such and such a time, watch out. Do not threaten him by suggesting that you will go on strike yourself if he doesn't get things done. Do not attempt to shame him in front of family and friends in order to motivate him. Here is a thought for you if you are dealing with an unmotivated handyman. I heard of one wife who said to her fully capable husband that if he wasn't going to get some specific things done around the house in a timely manner she was going to call a handyman in to do it. She got him motivated, not by guilt but by saving his money from being spent on an outside handyman.

> ෨෦෬
> IT IS NOT ONLY WHAT YOU SAY BUT HOW YOU SAY IT THAT SETS THE ATMOSPHERE IN YOUR HOUSE.

Do not try to be his mother, i.e., scolding, yelling, and disciplining him. This will definitely not create a positive atmosphere in your home. My husband says he only needs one mother and I am not her!

Pressure points are all over our bodies and we all have a significant number of them. Some people call them "hot buttons." Do you know your husband's "hot buttons"? For some men it's traffic jams, a messy house, taking a shot at his mother, letting the kids play in his office, et cetera. Avoid hot buttons as much as you can, especially when you want to ask for something special. Pressure points are places that produce pain. These sore spots are like land mines that are hidden to the naked eye. A wise wife steps around her husband's sore spots and meets him on solid ground as she presents her wishes. A sore spot for my husband is when I say, "I told you so!" If I am right, he is smart enough to figure that out, I do not need to rub his face in it. Men are like machines! Push the wrong buttons and you will get the wrong results! Push the right buttons and you will get the right results.

Men are much more moody than they are willing to admit! Learn to read your husband's moods. Watch the way he is acting before you ask for the moon. Is he grumpy, grouchy, hungry, or happy? The Bible says in Ecclesiastes 3:7 (NIV) that there is "a time to be silent and a time to speak." Know what time and season you are in at all times. A farmer doesn't waste his seed sowing it in the winter time. He waits until the right time, during spring sowing season, to go ahead and sow his seed to maximize his results.

See his moods like a traffic light at a busy crossroad. If he is upset with his boss or others, it's an automatic red light. A yellow light might be that he has had a long day and is tired and hungry. Sometimes caution is thrown to the wind and we wives find ourselves running red lights instead of yellow lights. A green light is a man who is happy at work, happy with others, and sexually satisfied! That scenario might appear more difficult for you to see with your own eyes than a lunar eclipse! If you can't get all three lined up, two out of three is good in most cases.

Minding the mood swings of your husband, knowing his pressure points, and setting the right atmosphere are essential elements to learning the fine art of timing. As we time things better our marriages and lives will go better and we will save ourselves a lot of time and energy.

Sticking Points

❖ What are your husband's "hot buttons"?

❖ What are the essential elements to learning the fine art of timing?

❖ List three things you should NOT do to motivate your husband to do things you want him to do.

1._____

2._____

3._____

CHAPTER TWENTY

Tell Him What You Really Want

Walk straight, act right, tell the truth.

Psalm 15:2 (The Message)

Most men do not do well picking up on subtle hints when conversing with their wives. There are a slew of reasons why we women don't ask for things more directly. Sometimes it is because we want to see just how well our man is listening. Other times it is that we don't want our request rejected so we do not pose a yes or no question but rather give him a suggestion. The power of suggestion may work for some men, but it is like subliminal advertisement for most. You just don't see great results! Another reason is we don't want to appear pushy or start an argument. We desire our men to know us and make an effort to pick up on our needs by responding when we drop hints. Our lack of results may simply be that there is a very real difference in the communication styles of men and women, not that they don't care about us.

From the time we are in our mother's womb to the tomb, men and women are different. Neuroscientists have known for many years that the brains of men and women are not identical. Men's brains tend to be more lateralized—that is, the two hemispheres operate more independently during specific mental tasks like speaking or navigating around one's environment. For the same kinds of tasks, females tend to use both their cerebral hemispheres more equally. This may help explain why men tend to be so logical and often-times not in touch with their feelings. Some men are plain and simple in an "emotional coma" and are in need of artificial life support from their wives. My husband and I have done quite a lot of foreign travel and one thing we noticed rather quickly was if we couldn't speak the language it was very difficult to communicate. Whatever country you are in you must learn their language if you are going to get anything accomplished. John Grey's book says, "Men are from Mars and women are from Venus!" If we are not from different planets we are at least from different countries and speak different languages. Men think in terms of bold-print headlines, women think in terms of the fine-print details. Details many times bore men, but they excite women. My husband tells me so-and-so had a baby. End of story. I want to know if it was a boy or a girl, the baby's name, weight, length, how was the labor, et cetera. Genders think and communicate differently. The average man speaks only about one-half the number of words a typical women does in a day. (By the time the average man gets home from work he has met most of his quota and his wife is just getting started.)

> ℬℭℜ
> FROM THE TIME WE ARE IN OUR MOTHER'S WOMB TO THE TOMB, MEN AND WOMEN ARE DIFFERENT.

When you are trying to communicate with your husband imagine you are in a different country and you will be alright. His language may be foreign to you but if you are going to get results you need to learn to speak his language. Cut to the chase and tell him what you want if you really want it.

After twenty-five years of marriage, a friend of mine shared with me how she has learned over the years to "go direct." Her husband is a successful dentist and real estate investor and yet she has learned that hints do not help. Telling her husband that she wanted jewelry was not enough. She got a Kaufmanns department store catalogue, circled the jewelry she wanted, and put her name by it. The direct approach may not seem very romantic but it gets the job done and makes life a lot easier for your husband. Men don't like to play a guessing game when it comes to getting you what you want or need, so let him know your heart's desire.

There was a time when I needed a particular type of perfume so I walked my husband down to the store and showed him exactly which perfume I was looking for. He told me he would have purchased the wrong one if I hadn't pointed out what I wanted. He will surprise me later with the timing and the way in which he presents it to me! You can save yourself much frustration and your husband a lot of running around by simply telling him in his language just what you want!

STICKING POINTS

❖ Why don't women ask for things more directly?

❖ How do you and your husband differ in communication styles?

❖ How can you communicate better with your husband?

CHAPTER TWENTY-ONE

Make a Good Report List

I'll make a list of GOD's gracious dealings,
all the things GOD has done that need praising,
All the generous bounties of GOD,
his great goodness to the family of Israel—
Compassion lavished, love extravagant.

Isaiah 63:7 (The Message)

More women report marital dissatisfaction than men. But more marriages dissolve when men say they are dissatisfied than when women say they are discontented. I believe that women have higher expectations and more patience than men in general. Women also may possess more faith. When a man marries he looks at his bride and says I hope she never changes, but when a woman marries she believes that she can change him. Some days it's obvious why we got married and some days we are left wondering why we ever said, "I do."

A woman was walking in the street when she heard a voice, "Stop! Stand still! If you take one more step, a brick will fall down on your head and kill you." The woman stopped and a big brick fell right in front of her. The woman was astonished. She went on and after awhile she was going to cross the road. Once again the voice shouted, "Stop! Stand still! If you take one more step a car will run over you and you will die." The woman did as she was instructed and a car came careening around the corner, barely missing her. "Where are you?" the woman asked. "Who are you?" "I am your guardian angel," the voice answered. "Oh yeah?" the woman asked. "And where were you when I got married?"

We all have some days when we feel like our guardian angel let their guard down on the day we got married. Those are the days we especially need to have our *Good Report List* out and ready to read and receive. A good report list is based upon a life-changing Bible verse found in Philippians 4:8 (NIV), "Finally, brothers, whatever is true, whatever is noble, whatever is right, whatever is pure, whatever is lovely, whatever is admirable—if anything is excellent or praiseworthy—think about such things." As much as we would love to have him or find him there is no perfect husband! We can find fault in every man including our husbands without much effort. Babe Ruth struck out twice as many times as he hit home runs but fans choose to remember him for his home runs not his strikeouts. Make it your goal to be your husband's number one fan and remember him for his best qualities and not his worst.

> ℰℭ
> REMEMBER HIM FOR HIS BEST QUALITIES AND NOT HIS WORST.

To be your husband's number one cheerleader you have to know what you are cheering about. I have been to a lot of sporting events in my life and I have never ever heard one single cheerleader booing their own team. Marriage is a team event and whether we like it or not as long as we are married we are on the same team. Mark my words, a number of dynamic changes will transpire when you create your husband's *Good Report List* and use it to focus on what he is doing right rather than what he is doing wrong. Start out with one or two of his top qualities such as, 1) He is a good provider, 2) He works hard, et cetera. It may take you a few hours or even days to come up with your top ten list but keep working on it. Remember the things he does to demonstrate his love toward you and your children if you have any. A top ten list may look something like this:

1. He is a good provider.
2. He works hard.
3. He tells me he loves me.
4. He takes me out when I am tired or need a break.
5. He listens to me when I whine.
6. He is funny and fun to be with.
7. He plays with the children.
8. He helps around the house.
9. He remembers my birthday and our anniversary.
10. He gives me flowers and other gifts to romance me.

This list does not define a perfect man but a man who has a number of admirable traits that many men do not possess. Here is what you will find while you are writing your list: First of all, you will discover that you are not married to the son of Satan. His bad attributes will start to fade as you highlight his good ones. Secondly, you will become motivated to look for more of his good traits. Thirdly, your motivation to love him back and your energy level in general will dramatically rise as you think positive thoughts about the man you chose to marry. And fourth, you will become a much happier, satisfied person yourself. A husband's good report list will spill over into other areas of your life so that your thanksgiving will turn into thanks living!

STICKING POINTS

❖ What are the four things you will discover while writing your list?

❖ How can you become more satisfied in your marriage?

❖ List the top ten "Good Report" things about your husband.

CHAPTER TWENTY-TWO

Keep Improving Yourself

And set your minds and keep them set on
what is above (the higher things),
not on the things that are on the earth.

Colossians 3:2 (AMP)

One of the biggest marriage wreckers today is when couples grow apart because one spouse is growing and developing and the other spouse is not! One of the best lines of defense against the potential "other woman" is to keep your husband focused on you by periodically and purposefully improving yourself. Sometimes we have a false impression that husbands want to have their wives stay the same. While some husbands may want 100 percent predictability, many want to be married to a woman who keeps improving herself. Every marriage is different. In some marriages, the husband is a mover and shaker and sprints out ahead of his wife vocationally, educationally, socially, spiritually, et cetera. In other cases it is the wife who gets the jump-start and leaves her husband in the dust. I am married to a type A personality who never stops pushing forward and I would like to share with you some valuable insights to help you strike a healthy balance in your marriage.

They say there are three words in real estate: location, location, location. Well there are three words in marriage as well: communication, communication, communication. Talk about your "growth expectations." If your husband wants to get a master's degree, what does that mean for you? Does he expect you to follow suit or do you have reason to acquire a master's degree? Competition may be very healthy in business but not in marriage. Do not compete with your spouse about who is the smartest or the highest paid. I know a lady who was married to a great all-around guy. He was the whole package but she made more money than he did and constantly reminded him of her superior earning abilities. Sad to say, that couple is not married today. Her constant monetary harassment definitely undercut his ego and their marriage. Before one partner launches out to further develop him or herself, the decent thing to do is to talk about how the change will impact everyone involved. That way you will minimize the side effects of the forward move. Learn to celebrate your spouse's accomplishments rather than compete against him. You are on the same team!

Be real about what common ground and common desires you both possess. Paul and I love to hike up high in picturesque mountains. We have been to gorgeous peaks in Estes Park in Colorado, the Grand Tetons in Wyoming, and the breathtaking Nepali Gast in Hawaii. We developed this sporting adventure together. Paul tried to get me to golf with him but he didn't have the patience to watch the many practice swings for each shot. We swim together but I don't body-surf like he does. I love spending hours assembling creative memory books, but he just enjoys looking at the finished project. We both decided to work out together to get into shape and we have stayed with it for over three and a half years. The point is, no couple will want to do everything together but if you are going to have a strong, healthy marriage you have to find a number of areas where you can grow together.

Growing as a couple is both spouses' responsibility! You must tell your husband what your growth and achievement priorities are and then listen to him tell you about his. Even if you are both in vastly different technical fields it is vitally important that your spouse understands and celebrates your life direction, goals, and dreams. If your spouse is pulling ahead in life, do not resent him, celebrate him! Make sure you perceive what he is doing and why he is doing it. If he seems to be distancing himself from you, do not tell him to stop his believing and achieving but do your best to support him and grow at least in your understanding, if not your skill base. If you find yourself lapping your spouse in life it may be that you need to slow down and bring him in the loop or risk losing touch with the love of your life. Marriage is a life partnership and it is a relationship meant for people who want to do life together and grow together!

> ෨෨෬
> IF YOU ARE GOING TO HAVE A STRONG, HEALTHY MARRIAGE YOU HAVE TO FIND A NUMBER OF AREAS WHERE YOU CAN GROW TOGETHER.

STICKING POINTS

❖ What are the three words in marriage that will keep you and your spouse on the same page?

1._____

2._____

3._____

❖ What are your "growth expectations" in marriage?

❖ Name three areas you and your spouse would like to improve on and make a plan to accomplish them.

MEN
STICKING EMOTIONALLY

CHAPTER TWENTY-THREE

Make Her Laugh

Bring a gift of laughter.

Psalm 100:2 (The Message)

I am convinced that girls love to laugh. I have three wonderful daughters and I have noticed that they are all attracted to guys that make them laugh. Laughter is good medicine for the soul and the Bible says, "A merry heart doeth good like a medicine" Proverbs 17:22 (KJV).

The first time I talked to Patti in our college cafeteria and then on our first date, we laughed together a lot. I believe that couples who laugh together stay together. Laughter has a way of soothing the soul and getting our focus off the negative and onto the positive. Laughter opens up the emotions and creates acceptance, warmth, and good will. There is a reason that top motivational speakers all use humor when they speak. They know it will endear the audience to them and the message they wish to convey.

> ಬಂಜ
> LAUGHTER OPENS UP THE
> EMOTIONS AND CREATES
> ACCEPTANCE, WARMTH,
> AND GOOD WILL.

Humor is motivational and it can help keep a troubled marriage afloat. What kind of humor is appropriate? Guys, you can laugh at yourself and laugh at others, but do not laugh at your lady or make her the brunt of your jokes. One nationally known evangelist almost ruined his marriage because he thought it was funny inciting others to laugh at his wife. He finally came to grips with his marriage-destroying behavior and cut his wife out of his humorous material and saved his marriage.

Patti and I really enjoy humorous preachers and conference speakers. We watch comedies and share funny stories because there is great bonding when we laugh together. We all seek to be around people who make us laugh. Being funny is not just inborn, but it can be learned over time. A common trait of most funny people is that they themselves love to laugh. Learn to laugh at yourself and stop being serious about everything. You can be very responsible and still see the lighter side of life. The Bible states that "the Lord laughs" (Psalm 37:13 NKJV). Jesus was extremely popular around children, which tells me that Jesus laughed a lot.

Another way to improve your humoring skill is to spend time with funny people. We become more and more like those we associate with. You can also learn to pick up on funny jokes and repeat them. There are no copyrights on jokes and it is always a good idea to have a few on hand.

"[There is] a time to weep and a time to laugh" (Ecclesiastes 3:4 NIV). Laughter is not always appropriate, but most of the time it bonds couples and opens us up emotionally to share more of ourselves with those we love. Good things happen in people who laugh because they know it is more important what happens in them than what happens to them.

STICKING POINTS

❖ Do you have humorous friends you can go out with that might help lighten things up?

❖ List three things you can do to have fun and laugh with your wife. Plan to do one a week for the next three weeks.

1._____

2._____

3._____

❖ Your challenge is simple: "Lighten up!"

CHAPTER TWENTY-FOUR

Surprise, Surprise, Surprise

He [God] stood me up on a wide-open field;
I stood there saved—surprised to be loved.

2 Samuel 22:20 (The Message)

When Patti and I were dating in college the other girls would collect in her room at night and ask her, "What did he do to surprise you?" Patti would then tell them about the times I had taken her on picnics, riding on the back of my motorcycle, or when I had given her flowers, handmade cards, or balloon bouquets.

After dating for one year (to the day), I surprised Patti by taking her out one night to an upscale restaurant in Tampa, Florida. Afterwards I took her to a secluded section of Clearwater Beach where I began to give her a series of gifts under the moonlit sky. The last gift was a heart-shaped, handmade card that had taken me one week to compose. The card itemized 101 reasons why I wanted her to marry me. On the other side of the card was written, "Will you marry me?"

She probably would have said no if she had known that the surprises would end for several years after our marriage. But, to her young heart, she readily accepted my invitation to marriage. Unbeknownst to her, I had tape recorded the entire episode, which included much giggling and lip smacking.

After getting married she was definitely in for a surprise—now the surprise gifts she received could be called "guilt offerings." Guilt offerings were what I brought to her when I was coming home late after work, far beyond the time I had told her I would be home. The "guilt offerings" included teddy bears, flowers, chocolates, and a variety of other small gifts, as I tried to appease her disappointment.

She was not very excited about receiving those gifts. What she wanted was me to be more focused on her instead of my many other new interests. Patti felt let down after we were married because all of the energy and creativity that I had put toward surprising her now seemed to be focused on my new position as a youth pastor and taking care of the kids and their needs.

From time to time she would suggest to me some nice, fun place to go just the two of us and I would say, "Oh, what a great place to take the youth!" which added more fuel to her disappointment. Many newly married men fall into this behavior pattern after they feel that they have won the love of their lives. They go on to new challenges at work or with hobbies or personal interests. It takes time to be creative and plan surprises that will add zest to any marriage.

Up until the last couple of years, I didn't realize how valuable surprises were to the enrichment of my marriage. Through much of my married years in my 20s and 30s I rarely surprised Patti. The exception would be occasionally for birthdays, such as on her 30th when I called together the staff at the church for a special luncheon and invited a gorilla to surprise her. The gorilla picked her up off the ground and embarrassed her more than surprised her. The gorilla poked through her hair, played with her face, and acted as though he was in love with her.

The important thing was that just because I personally wasn't into surprises did not mean that Patti wasn't. For instance, when family members would ask me what I wanted for my birthday or for Christmas, I would say "I don't know, I'll buy myself something and give you the receipt." Patti didn't just want me to give her money or gift certificates. She wanted me to take the time to find something that would be special and let her know how important she was to me.

Men, surprises do not have to be expensive. You can take time off work to take her out to lunch, call her during the day to tell her how much you are thinking about her, or send her a love card or flowers for no special occasion. In the winter warm up her car and scrape the windows for her before she goes out. Serve her breakfast in bed. Fill up the tank with gas and wash her car for her. And then, every once in awhile, especially on big occasions, you need to really blow her mind.

For Patti's 40th birthday, I decided to go all out. I planned a week-long list of surprises. It started with Sunday at church. When she drove up into the parking lot we had on the front sign of the church, "Happy 40th Birthday, Patti" and on one entrance a sign saying, "Hogs and Kisses" with dozens of yard signs of little pigs and at the other entrance there were pink flamingos everywhere. I sang her *Happy Birthday* in front of the entire congregation (they sang too) and the congregation gave her cards and gifts and we had a beautiful birthday cake.

Then after service, I told Patti that we weren't going home. I took her to downtown Cleveland to the Ritz Carleton Hotel to stay overnight, where I gave her a gorgeous tanzanite ring, which happens to be her favorite gemstone, after the diamond of course. The next day, I took her shopping at two malls. I bought her some tanzanite earrings and numerous articles of clothing. The following night, I hired a chef to come to the house to prepare one of her favorite meals.

For the grand finale, I took her out to dinner. Unbeknownst to her, I had secretly invited a group of forty of our friends. When she arrived everyone yelled, "Surprise" and sang *Happy Birthday* to her. Special guests in the group were her mother and father from Boston and her grandparents from West Virginia. Roses were at all the tables and I presented to her a bouquet of forty roses. I also hired some chamber musicians to play background music. For hours her family and friends shared, one after another, stories of how much Patti meant to them.

Sad to say I was attempting to make up for lost time! Most wives wouldn't be nearly as patient as Patti was. I surprised her before she heard wedding bells but dropped the ball, especially during the first years of your marriage. Remember, surprises do not end with the wedding ceremony; they should begin with it and never end!

STICKING POINTS

❖ Ask yourself, when was the last time you blew your wife's mind with a special surprise, other than for her birthday or on a holiday?

❖ What are two creative, not necessarily expensive, ways you can surprise your wife? Write them down and put a date next to them as to when you will surprise her.

1._____

2._____

CHAPTER TWENTY-FIVE

Build up Her Self-Esteem

Let thy fountain be blessed:
and rejoice with the wife of thy youth.
Let her be as the loving hind and pleasant roe;
let her breasts satisfy thee at all times;
and be thou ravished always with her love.

Proverbs 5:18-19 (KJV)

Years ago, Focus on the Family did a women's survey among married women between the ages of twenty-seven and forty years of age. The majority of these women had children and they were Christian, middle class, suburban housewives. They were asked to rank the following sources of depression in their lives:

- Absence of romantic love in marriage
- In-law conflict
- Low self-esteem
- Problems with the children
- Financial difficulties
- Loneliness, isolation, and boredom
- Sexual problems in marriage
- Menstrual and physiological problems
- Fatigue and time pressure
- Aging

In both the Focus on the Family survey and an exact same survey used among five thousand women at a Family Life Seminar, the most troubling problem of those listed was low self-esteem. Over 50 percent of the ladies marked "Low self-esteem" as their number-one problem and 80 percent put it among their top five problems.

Most women I have met suffer from some type of self-esteem problem. Many are into "Barbie bondage," thinking they are too fat, too skinny, too short, too tall, too ugly, too stupid, et cetera. In today's world that says image is everything, women are struggling to be beautiful enough, smart enough, and tough enough to compete. A poor self-esteem is so common among women that one can almost assume their wife needs to have her self-esteem worked on. Even a woman with a strong self-esteem should have her husband build her up. Psychologists tell us that over 90 percent of our self image comes from what we believe others think of us.

First and foremost, I believe the ultimate source of a healthy self-esteem is having a relationship with God, who valued all of us so much that He sent His Son to live with us and then die for us. Our image of how God perceives us is the most important ingredient to having a healthy self-esteem. The good news is that God loves us unconditionally and knows everything there is to know about our past, present, and future. Our self-esteem is often rooted in a twisted mindset of how God and others perceive us. "Feminine depression" can take many forms. Many females feel ugly or sexually unattractive, lonely, empty, or unloved and wish they were someone else.

A husband can make or break his wife's self-esteem by the words he says or doesn't say. The Bible states that "Death and life are in the power of the tongue" (Proverbs 18:21 NKJV). A wise husband will speak life into his wife.

Many fail to notice that the major reason why the Proverbs 31 woman is such an extraordinary woman. "Her children rise up and call her blessed; her husband also, and he praises her: 'Many daughters have done well, But you excel them all'" (Proverbs 31:28-29 NKJV). Husbands, your words can make the difference between "feminine depression" and a strong self-confidence displayed in your wife. Many foolish men have battered their wives with their words and wondered why their wives are depressed, aloof, and sexually unexciting. The problem may be your failure to speak positive words of faith and words of life into her life. When we build someone else up, we will reap what we sow.

> ℘ℂ℘
>
> HUSBANDS, YOUR WORDS CAN MAKE THE DIFFERENCE BETWEEN "FEMININE DEPRESSION" AND A STRONG SELF-CONFIDENCE DISPLAYED IN YOUR WIFE.

Let your wife hear many times a day that you love her, that she is "the bomb," and that you are enthralled with her love and you will feel better about her and yourself in the long run.

STICKING POINTS

❖ Ask yourself, do you build up or tear down your wife's self-esteem?

❖ Start complimenting your wife at every opportunity and see how it affects her self-image, demeanor, attitude, et cetera.

❖ Take notice of how many positive and negative things you say to her throughout the day and at home. Instead of just making a list of five things you need to start saying, you also need to make a list of five things you need to stop saying.

CHAPTER TWENTY-SIX

Fulfill Her Emotional Needs

You husbands in the same way,
live with your wives in an understanding way,
as with someone weaker, since she is a woman;
and show her honor as a fellow heir of the grace of life,
so that your prayers will not be hindered.

1 Peter 3:7 (NASB)

When conducting marriage counseling one of the most common complaints I hear from wives is that "he is not fulfilling my emotional needs." Most men are clueless when it comes to filling their wife's emotional gas tanks. After Mel Gibson starred in the movie *What Women Want* he was asked, "Now that you've done the movie, can you tell us what women want?" and he said, "I have no idea."

Meeting a woman's emotional needs may be a husband's number one marital challenge. This is much more of an art than a science. Every woman has a different set of emotional needs that are ever changing. When their emotional needs are not being met at home, she is a prime target for an affair.

I helped a friend save her marriage and nationally known ministry. At the beginning she found herself emotionally charged by a man that she was working with. Most affairs begin with an emotional bond (emotional adultery) that later leads to a physical bond. That's why it is so essential that you safeguard your marriage by building an emotional bridge to your wife that you travel across often.

Begin with becoming an active listener. Experts tell us that 85 percent of our learning is derived from listening. The problem is that most listeners admit they are distracted, preoccupied, or forget what they have heard 75 percent of the time. According to the Internal Listening Web site, people listen at about 120-250 words per minute but they can think at about 1,000-3,000 words per minute. Listening requires your attention.

Women generally communicate their emotional needs more subtly than men do. Wives often drop hints when they say, "We have not gone out for quite awhile." That means it is time to make a dinner reservation or plan a date night. If she says, "The kids are driving me crazy," that means it is time for you to take charge. Sometimes she will ask to be held and sometimes she will ask not to be held. When you respond accordingly you are meeting her emotional needs.

The hints she drops may be clear to you or they may appear like a secret code. The key is to correctly decipher the messages she is sending you. Remembering details, her likes and dislikes, emotionally charges your wife. If I know that Patti hates green peppers and bring home a pizza with a green pepper topping, I can guarantee that the emotional climate will change from bright and sunny to severe thunderstorms.

One line that Patti hates is "I forgot." She says that is a childish excuse! When you are an adult, Patti says a man needs to remember. It took me nearly ten years to remember that Patti didn't want crème-filled chocolates on Valentine's Day and other special occasions. She loves chocolates with lots of nuts and caramel. It took me some fifteen years to figure out that birthdays, anniversaries, and even holidays needed to be celebrated on the appropriate day!

It took me many years to learn that there is a big, big difference between my laughing at Patti and my laughing with Patti. When your wife says she is cooking a very nice meal, be home for dinner and on time. I never cease to be amazed at how my wife can be in a happy mood one minute and then be reminded of something I did to her years ago and her mood suddenly shifts gears and we go from forward to reverse.

When you don't listen to your wife you can be sure that you will not be meeting her emotional needs. I took Patti to the 2002 Winter Olympics to see the figure skating finals, which was an emotional high for her. On the last day of the trip I took her snowmobiling in a remote region near the border of Wyoming and Utah. She was having a blast until I decided to take the snowmobile off the trail, ignoring her words of wisdom to stay on the trail. Well, when I got the snow-mobile stuck in a six-foot snowdrift eight miles away from any other human being it was like taking an emotional wrecking ball to our romantic getaway. I could have avoided a lot of emotional turmoil by just listening to Patti! Emotionally distraught women are rarely married to good listeners who adjust to meet the emotional needs of their wives.

I have enjoyed sailing for almost thirty-five years. One thing I learned a long time ago is that you must adjust to the ever-changing wind patterns. Your wife's emotional needs will shift. What worked yesterday may not work today at all and so you must adjust.

Never underestimate the significance of meeting your wife's emotional needs as many women will put this at the top of their list when rating their marriage. Decode the encrypted messages, listen to her actively and attentively, and act on both your present and past knowledge and you will make your life and wife a lot happier than you ever dreamed possible.

STICKING POINTS

❖ Listen closely to what your wife tells you. What clues are you overlooking that might better help you fulfill her emotional needs?

❖ Find three ways that you can better understand and meet your wife's emotional needs. Practice them this week!

1._____

2._____

3._____

WOMEN
STICKING EMOTIONALLY

CHAPTER TWENTY-SEVEN

Be His Number One Cheerleader

Therefore encourage one another and build each other up.

1 Thessalonians 5:11 (NIV)

There is a reason why almost every sports team has cheerleaders! Cheerleaders help bring out the best in the team. As a wife, I realize that my husband needs to be encouraged just as much during hard times as when everything seems to be going his way. Here are a couple of ways you can be your husband's number one cheerleader:

1. Applaud his accomplishments.
    While the pastor of the world's largest church, Dr. Paul Younggi Cho, was speaking at a church in Pensacola, Florida, he said that his wife never would compliment him after he preached. He had many others who spoke highly of his messages but his wife never would. One day he came home from church and confronted her and asked her, "Why don't you ever compliment my preaching?" She responded, "You have plenty of other people complimenting you all the time, and I didn't want

to make you prideful." He told her that the other people's compliments meant little to him but it was her opinion that he valued and needed most. She learned that her husband, even though he pastored the largest church in the world, needed her to be his number one cheerleader. Never take your husband's accomplishments for granted.

My husband is rarely down or depressed but when he is I've learned to remind him of his many accomplishments. One time, we bought a house as an investment at a sheriff's sale and started to do thousands of dollars of work rehabbing the house, only to be suddenly informed that the sale was null and void because of an error made by the sheriff's department. Paul was not only down about the potential loss of rehab money and profit, but the countless hours of work we put into getting the house ready for occupancy.

> ❧
> MAKE IT YOUR GOAL TO INFLATE, NOT DEFLATE, HIS SELF-ESTEEM BY THE PRAISEFUL WORDS YOU SPEAK TO HIM.

I didn't let him forget his other real estate, business, ministry, and family accomplishments at that critical time in our lives. We prayed about it and the sheriff's department ended up fixing their error and proceeding with the sale.

Put milestones by your husband's successes. When the people of God passed through the Jordan en route to the Promised Land, God had them set up twelve stones on the riverbank to serve as a constant reminder of their past successes. Focusing on what your husband has done instead of what he hasn't can prove to be a valuable steppingstone through the storms of life. Make it your goal to inflate, not deflate, his self-esteem by the praiseful words you speak to him.

2. Encourage your husband.
   To encourage means to cheer, comfort, inspire, boost, invigorate, put one on top of the world, rejoice the heart, and do the heart good. Talk about a recipe for marital success. Everyone wants to be around people who make them feel good about themselves. Start the day off right. If you are not a morning person, limit your words until you can say something positive! I have noticed that if I am snippy with my husband in the morning it can boomerang back to me and add to the stress in both of our lives. If you know your husband has a big project, deal, or meeting during the day you can encourage him about it and believe for the best.

   Another way to put your husband at the top of the world is to sometimes tell him that you want to be intimate with him that evening. Just make sure that you follow through. Tell him when you are both fully dressed and walking out the door to work.

   You can transform your marriage with your words of encouragement. Men have a need to be needed. Tell him that you and others need him. When a man feels needed it really does motivate him. Make it a habit to brag about him in front of the family, your friends, and even strangers from time to time. Remind him often that you believe in him and in his abilities to accomplish incredible things in life.

STICKING POINTS

❖ What areas of your husband's life can you applaud?

❖ What is the definition of encouragement?

❖ Name two things you can do each day to encourage your husband.

1._____

2._____

CHAPTER TWENTY-EIGHT

Appreciate Your Husband's God-Given Personaltiy

Be devoted to each other like a loving family.
Excel in showing respect for each other.

Romans 12:10 (GWT)

You say, "What personality?" Every man has a personality. One of the things that helped me in our marriage was learning about my husband's personality traits. God not only wired men and women differently both mentally and emotionally, but He also gave us different gifts and personality types.

There are four basic personalities and you need to know which one your husband possesses. I suggest you read one or both of these excellent books on this pertinent subject: *Temperament* by Dr. Tim LaHaye and *Four Personalities* by Sandy Kulkin. Dr. Kulkin has identified the four basic personality types as: D-I-S-C.

My husband and I have two totally different personalities. He is a "D" (Driven) and I am an "S" (Stable, Steady) personality. Even when we are on vacation he wants to do everything there is to do and see everything there is to see, all the while he is dragging me along with him. One summer we went to Sedona,

Arizona with some friends. Paul took us on a back-country Jeep ride in the desert in the middle of the day. Then he wanted to go hiking for the next couple of hours. Our friends said, "You go right ahead and have your hike. We will go down the street to this cute little café and relax while we enjoy the scenery and have lunch." I was so hungry and hot that the last thing I wanted to do was go hiking! Once I discovered the limits of his personality and mine, I learned that he wasn't trying to kill me with his boundless energy and activities.

Paul's family calls him "The Activity God." One time we were on vacation in Jamaica with our four-month son, Gideon. Hotel employees and guests repeatedly came up to me to ask where Paul was because they wanted to play various sports with him. After a few days of watching Paul go from one activity to the next, one lady said to me that he was keeping them all entertained!

Opposites often attract in personality styles. This is not necessarily a bad thing. It is much easier to comple-ment each other when you aren't Siamese twins. Having different personality types can help you both compensate for your individual blind spots and weaknesses. My husband needs me to help him see the way

> ෨෬
> BALANCE IS A KEY TO A SUCCESSFUL LIFE AND MARRIAGE AND VARIOUS PERSONALITIES CAN COUNTER-BALANCE ONE ANOTHER FOR THE COMMON GOOD.

individuals may be affected by his vision. I need him to see the big picture of where we can be in five, ten, or twenty years! Balance is a key to a successful life and marriage and various personalities can counterbalance one another for the common good.

Every personality has its strengths and weaknesses. Openly discuss the chinks in your armor and let your partner cover for you if at all possible. You and your spouse may be in the same house, the same room, and even the same bed for years but until you discover the power of your individual personalities it is very possible that you could be living miles apart! Knowledge is power. When you tap into the power of your personalities through natural disclosure it will help you both better understand and love each other. By knowing your personality differences you can avoid many frustrations in your marriage.

Once you know what to expect it can actually be quite entertaining for both of you! My husband and I now know what our personality patterns are because we have become students of our own and one another's personality types. Use your personalities and talents to complete one another instead of to *compete* with one another.

STICKING POINTS

❖ Do you see areas in which you and your spouse are opposites? List them.

❖ Look at the list. Do they help you see potential blind spots or weaknesses?

❖ The next time your spouse's personality starts to be a point of contention, make a decision to enjoy your differences and watch how his personality and talents will actually add to your relationship.

CHAPTER TWENTY-NINE

Be a Woman He Can Share His TNT With

Bear (endure, carry) one another's burdens and troublesome moral faults, and in this way fulfill and observe perfectly the law of Christ (the Messiah) and complete what is lacking [in your obedience to it].

Galatians 6:2 (AMP)

Now you might be wondering what is TNT? It stands for "Troubles and Temptations." We need to be women of faith with whom our husbands can share their inner troubles and temptations. If your husband knows you will fall apart if he tries to share his struggles with you, he won't come to you when he needs backup. All husbands go through TNT from time to time. He might be a great man but he is not super-human. Your husband should be able to come to you and find you speaking faith and love into his life. You do not have to understand but you do need to encourage him.

> ∞∞
> YOUR HUSBAND SHOULD BE ABLE TO COME TO YOU AND FIND YOU SPEAKING FAITH AND LOVE INTO HIS LIFE.

I heard of a prominent businessman who was going through tremendous pressure in his business. He came home down and depressed after losing a huge account and he wanted to talk about it. His wife shut him down saying she did not want to talk about it as her golf outing at the club had been rained out that day. That was the day he decided to divorce her. Men might not admit it, but they need a sounding board, a listening ear, and even a shoulder to cry on at times.

Men and women have profound differences in their mental and emotional makeup. Don't insist that your husband share his feelings with you if he doesn't want to or is not ready to do so. Men want to solve their problems by themselves and tend to think about their feelings before they open up and share them. As a woman, I want to talk about things, get advice from others, and share my feelings. Just be patient and know that when he is finally ready to "open up," you should be willing to drop everything and be there for him.

My husband and I love to go hiking in the mountains to enjoy God's great outdoors. From time to time we will hike through a valley that literally blocks out the sun for a time. Do we stop? Do we camp there? No, we press on through together. Husbands sometimes go through emotional valleys, career valleys, or financial valleys and your encouraging words, or simply your attention, can help lift their loads and dispel the darkness.

My husband tells others that his best ideas are mine. I don't know if I completely agree with that but because I have listened, praised, and asked God for wisdom we have received some breakthrough ideas together. If I had just told him to go for a drive or walk and "deal with it" by himself when he was troubled about something we wouldn't have the deep bond that we have today. Sports teams that come from behind to win the big ones have a lasting bond and many good memories. Build a bond and make a memory with your husband by walking with him through the inevitable deep, dark valleys of life!

All men are tempted! If Jesus Christ was tempted in every way so will your husband and mine be tempted. Paul and I heard of a couple where the husband had thirteen affairs. He was living a double life and not being honest about his temptations with his wife. Temptations thrive in secret, dark places. Once they are brought out into the light they tend to shrivel up. Believe it or not they went from a "closed marriage" to an "open marriage" after the thirteen affairs because he now talked to his wife about his inner struggles and temptations. As far as we know, that couple is still together because they both decided to be open and honest with God and one another about their temptations. This open-door policy for wives can literally help to affair-proof your marriage and deepen your love for one another.

If more women would stand by their man "before the fall" instead of afterwards, I believe many affairs and divorces could be avoided. Your standing with him through his TNT can "blow away" the other woman that may be lurking in the shadows and help your husband to know you are his best friend. Best friends talk about everything and they bring out the best in one another. Deep disclosure lays the groundwork for forever friendship and marriages that will last a life-time!

Sticking Points

❖ Do you feel your faith is at a level that your husband can share his troubles and temptations with you?

❖ Don't wait for your husband to share his TNT with you. Ask him how his work is going or how a certain problem is . . . then just listen or add your wisdom to it.

MEN
STICKING SEXUALLY

CHAPTER THIRTY

Eyes Only for Her

Keep your eyes straight ahead;
ignore all sideshow distractions.

Proverbs 4:25 (The Message)

Recently, a young lady in our church's singles ministry started dating a guy from the same singles ministry. I asked her after the first date how she liked him. Her immediate response was negative, "He was looking at other girls." She not only could tell me which girls he was looking at but even the part of their bodies he was looking at.

Not only do women notice other women, but they are also very aware of guys who are checking out other women. Of course it's okay for your wife to notice another woman's beauty or curves, but you take your life in your own hands if you do the same. It is hard not to look at members of the opposite sex and live on planet Earth, but the key is to never eyeball a woman.

Awhile ago, my father and I were driving alone in my car and I passed a pretty girl riding a bike and I asked my seventy-plus-year-old dad, "Dad, do you still look at girls?" He came back with a response that said it all when he said, "I love your mother." I realized that he noticed women but never let it affect his love for his wife. Jesus said that "whoever looks at a woman to lust for her has already committed adultery with her in his heart" (Matthew 5:28 NIV). I told a middle-aged single man (who lived a playboy lifestyle before he became a Christian) that he needed to avoid looking at other women, especially when he was with his new Christian girlfriend that he was trying to impress and pursue. My strategy is working. She loves the focused attention and he is training himself to be the spiritual leader in their home, should they get married.

A woman, whether she is a wife, fiancée, or girlfriend, instinctively knows that she does not have the heart of a man who cannot control his reckless eyeballing of other women. Adultery of the heart, and sexually as well, often starts for a man after a second and third look. In the Bible, King David was having trouble sleeping one night. When he went out on the rooftop of the palace to get some fresh air, he saw beautiful Bathsheba taking a bath. If he would have turned his head after the first look, he would have saved himself and his family untold grief. We would have a totally different story to tell future generations about a "blameless man" who had a heart for God. Job is described in the Bible as a blameless man and he actually made a little pact with God. "I have made a

> **A WOMAN INSTINCTIVELY KNOWS THAT SHE DOES NOT HAVE THE HEART OF A MAN WHO CANNOT CONTROL HIS RECKLASS EYBALLING OF OTHER WOMEN.**

covenant with my eyes; Why then should I look upon a young woman?" Job 31:1 (NKJV).

Fathers, not only will your sins find you out but your sons will find out your sins as well. Some 70 percent of pornography gets into the hands of children. One of the basic needs of a woman is to have a sense of security. If a woman knows her man has eyes only for her, her sense of security is greatly heightened and she is actually freer to give herself completely to him. When the young lady at the beginning of the chapter saw roaming eyeballs, she put the brakes on the relationship. Remember, both God and your wife are watching your eyes and neither will bless you if you are recklessly eyeballing other women. I sometimes purposely turn my head and look directly at Patti when I see a "hot babe" coming our way and, believe me, that kind of behavior not only helps Patti to feel more secure but fortifies me spiritually.

STICKING POINTS

❖ Honestly rate yourself on a scale from 1-10, 10 being the greatest. How much do you struggle with reckless eyeballing?

❖ Make every attempt to look elsewhere when a sensuous looking woman is coming your way.

❖ Make a covenant with your eyes to not look upon a woman (Job 31:1).

CHAPTER THIRTY-ONE

Nonsexual Touching

Be kindly affectionate one to another.

Romans 12:10 (NKJV)

Affectionate touching is foreplay in a man's mind, but it is a sign of true love, tenderness, and emotional intimacy in a woman's mind.

Several years ago a lady wrote in to Ann Landers and said, "If you were to ask one hundred women how they feel about sexual intercourse ninety-eight would say, 'Just hold me close and be tender, forget about the act.' If you don't believe it, why not take a poll." So Ann Landers did just that, she asked a simple question of her readership, "Would you be content to be held close and treated tenderly and forget about the act of sex? Answer yes or no and please add one line, I am over or under forty years of age." Within a few months she had received over ninety thousand responses, making it the biggest response she had ever had to any question. It beat the meatloaf recipe, the lemon pie, and the poll asking parents, "If you had to do it over again, would you have children?" More than ninety thousand women cast their ballots. Seventy-two percent said yes, they would be content to be held close and treated tenderly and forget about the act. Of those 72 percent, 42 percent were under forty.

Here are some of the actual respondents to this big question. From Columbus, Ohio a woman says, "I'm under forty and would be delighted to settle for tender words and warm caresses. The rest of it is a bore and can be exhausting. I'm sure the sex act was designed strictly for the pleasure of males." From Westport, Connecticut a woman says, "I vote yes. My husband is a diabetic and hasn't been able to perform for ten years. I would have voted yes twenty years ago. He never bothered to satisfy me when he had his health. His illness was a blessing." Chicago, Illinois, "I don't want either his tender words or the act. My husband became impotent ten years ago due to alcoholism. The only words I want from him are 'Good-bye,' but the bum won't leave." Texarkana, Texas wrote, "Yes, without the tender embrace the act is animalistic. For years I hated sex and I felt used. I was relieved when my husband died. My present mate is on heart pills that have made him impotent. It's like heaven to be held and cuddled." Eureka, California wrote, "I am sixty-two and voting no. If my old man was over the hill I would settle for high school necking, but as long as he is able to shake the walls and wake up the neighbors downstairs, I want to get in on the action. And I'll take an encore anytime I can get it."

A woman who is treated considerately in her overall needs would probably sound more like the last lady than the others, but the fact remains that nonsexual touching is very high on the majority of most women's wish lists.

Let's start off with handholding. Patti and I took it very slow in the physical realm in our dating days! We didn't even hold hands for about a month after our courtship began. I can still remember the thrill that we both experienced going from the college chapel holding hands over to the school cafeteria. I have never stopped holding her hand because it keeps us close as a couple and it also keeps me from walking faster than her when we are out.

Husbands, it is important that you realize your wife is not a sexual machine. To most women, romance and sex are two different experiences. She likes the handholding and hugging. Most of the time a hug should not lead to sex. Patti loves it when I simply play with her hair. Nonsexual touching like that makes your wife feel loved and cherished. Prove to her how self-controlled you are and how much you love her as a person by affectionately touching her without expecting any sex at all.

Husbands, think "subtle" when you think of affectionate touching that will touch your wife's soul as well as her body. Most men are better at "mauling" their wives then affectionately touching her. Too many husbands aren't considerate or affectionate in public, but the minute the bedroom door is shut, the grabbing and groping begins. Your wife doesn't want to be slapped on the rear end as you would slap a buddy for making a touchdown in a football game.

Here is what may melt the ice with your wife:

- ◆ Brushing or playing with her hair
- ◆ Nibbling or whispering softly in her ear

+ Kissing the back of her neck
+ Massaging her shoulders, hands, or feet

Dr. James Dobson of Focus on the Family says, "A woman's need for emotional fulfillment is just as pressing and urgent as the physiological requirement for sexual release in the male."

> ℘)℃℞
> DR. JAMES DOBSON OF FOCUS ON THE FAMILY SAYS, "A WOMAN'S NEED FOR EMOTIONAL FULFILLMENT IS JUST AS PRESSING AND URGENT AS THE PHYSIOLOGICAL REQUIREMENT FOR SEXUAL RELEASE IN THE MALE."

In twenty years of counseling couples I have only once encountered a marriage where the wife wanted sex more than her husband. She wanted it every day. Sorry guys, she has already been taken. The vast majority of wives (under normal circumstances) don't want sex every day, but they do want nonsexual touching each and every day.

STICKING POINTS

❖ When was the last time you just held your wife with no strings attached?

❖ List three ways you can be affectionate with your wife this week without going for a touchdown.

1._____

2._____

3._____

CHAPTER THIRTY-TWO

Romeo, Romeo—Where Art Thou?

And it came to pass, when he had been there a long time, that Abimelech King of the Philistines looked out at a window, and saw, and, behold, Isaac was sporting with Rebekah his wife.

Genesis 26:8 (KJV)

A recent survey of women found that they fantasize about romance more than anything else and, most often, a romantic interlude with their own husbands! While men are visual in nature and only need to be aroused physically, women by and large need to be aroused emotionally first, then physically.

If the truth be told, most men suffer severely from RDD (Romantic Deficit Disorder). Romance is just as important to the well-being of a woman as sex is to a man. If she doesn't "get it" at home she may very well look for it elsewhere. Grocery stores know this and often provide bare-chested men on the covers of raunchy romance novels to lure romantically deprived women.

> ROMANCE IS JUST AS IMPORTANT TO THE WELL-BEING OF A WOMAN AS SEX IS TO A MAN.

Worse yet, I have had two wives from our church meet men romantically via the internet for a romantic rendezvous. One left her marriage and one stayed, but both weren't getting their romance needs met at home.

Here is a romance "starter kit" of five things every husband can do to light the fires of romance in his marriage.

Remember important dates, i.e., wedding anniversary, her birthday, the day you proposed, your first date, Valentine's Day, Sweetest Day, et cetera. A study was done and found that younger couples in their 20s spend around $160 on Valentine's Day whereas couples in their 30s and 40s spend half that much. One lady commented, "My birthday is on Valentine's Day; he forgot both." We should not be getting lazier with the one we love but we should be getting better. Romance requires a great memory and the closer to total recall, the better.

A good meal goes a long way! Patti and I were watching a man-on-the-street interview on a late night show. The interviewer was asking guys what their idea of a romantic dinner at home would be. One guy said he would order out Pizza Hut and some beers to romance a woman. He wasn't married or even close to getting there. Atmosphere is everything! A candlelit dinner with some nice music and good food is great, but it is not always necessary. It can be bright and colorful and have a Chinese Samurai chef lighting fires on your table instead of candlelight.

Romance requires creativity! Creatively loving your wife means finding many different ways to say, "I love you."

It may be a card, a kiss, a gift, a bouquet of flowers, a note under her pillow, an e-mail, personal love coupons you have designed to please her, et cetera. The secret to romance is—don't be predictable. It takes time to be romantic. It took me one week to personally handcraft the "101 reasons why I wanted Patti to marry me" card that I gave her the night I proposed to her. Variety is the spice of life and creative spouses don't repeat the "same old same old" over and over again.

Romance is not mechanical, it's spontaneous! It's going on a weekend getaway where you tell her Friday afternoon and have someone lined up to take care of the kids and everything else while you're away. Romance can be as simple as suddenly deciding to go down to the beach to see the sunset, taking her to her favorite ice-cream shop on a sweltering hot summer day, going for a bike ride to see the leaves change colors in the fall, or just taking a spontaneous walk in the park. In order to be spontaneous, you need to be flexible with your time, even if you have to schedule your "spontaneous time" with your spouse.

Romance requires sacrifice! Look at Romeo and Juliet, Anthony and Cleopatra, and many other classical love stories where there was no price too high to pay for true love. Please don't kill yourself for love, but the point is, sacrificial love is one of the most potent and powerful forms of romance. Patti's great-grandparents were originally from Lithuania. They were engaged to be married and both wanted to go to America. He went to America first. Patti's great-grandmother worked for three years, saving her money to get to America. Finally, the day came when she had enough money saved to book passage on a boat to New York. When she went to get her stash of money she had been hiding in her closet she found it had been taken by her brother. They had a very bad fight and she left the house. She managed to stow away on a boat to America. When she finally arrived in New York and found a job she sent word to her family to let them know where she was. When she received word from her family, she found out that her brother had been arrested for her murder and was awaiting trial. During the three plus years of separation, Patti's great-grandmother had lost contact with her fiancé. She finally met a family that she went to work for and moved with them to Michigan. There she found a young woman whom she became friends with that was also from Lithuania. There was a community of all Lithuanian people in Michigan and one night she was invited to a party with her friend. Her long-lost fiancé was at the party. After coming to America, he had married and had two small children. His wife had died shortly after the birth of the second child. Their romance rekindled and they married a few months later. How far will you go to show your spouse that you have counted the cost and are willing to pay the price to please them, protect them, provide for them, et cetera? Jesus Christ literally gave up His life for His bride (the Church) and as husbands we need to be willing to lay down our lives to sacrificially love and serve our wives.

Romance is a necessary ingredient for a healthy, happy marriage and it truly adds fuel to the fires of your love life. Husbands, with a little work and a lot of practice you can fulfill your wife's romantic fantasies and show her just how many ways you truly do love her!

STICKING POINTS

❖ Does your wife think you are romantic? On a scale of 1-10 how would she rate you?

❖ Find three ways to incorporate romance into your everyday life, not just on special occasions.

1._____

2._____

3._____

CHAPTER THIRTY-THREE

Don't Be a Deadhead after Sex

How beautiful is your love, my sister, my [promised] bride! How much better is your love than wine! And the fragrance of your ointments than all spices!

Song of Solomon 4:10 (AMP)

Patti and I went to Alaska during the summer of 2004 to see our fiftieth state together. We learned a lot about the habits of salmon while in Alaska. A man is much like a salmon. After he jumps through hoops over and over again in order to get his wife into bed with him and it has finally happened, he wants to turn over and die.

Let's face it. After a man has sex, he feels like a salmon. A salmon spawns, then rolls over and dies. After the typical man has sex, he flops over to his side of the bed, gasps for his last breath of air, and then slips into a deep sleep while his wife is wide awake and wants to bask in the afterglow. A smart and caring husband will resist the urge to rest.

An issue that often comes up during counseling with couples is what happens, or should I say what doesn't happen, after sex. In our highly sexualized world, information about sex is readily available, helping cause men and women to have higher expectations before, during, and after sex. The Tarzan and Jane days, where a man could beat his chest a few times and expect hot sex in the bedroom, are over.

Guys let's face it, there is a lot of work involved even in getting to the act of marriage. Husbands are lighting scented candles, running hot bathwater for bubble baths, and putting flowers and rose petals all over the bedroom in order to prepare the atmosphere for their wives. In addition to the "bedroom decorations" he may have already taken his wife to dinner, put on his best acts of chivalry, and told his wife five times more than normal that he loves her and that she looks beautiful.

Last impressions are often the ones that stick. When we hastily "finish our business" with our wives and head for our side of the bed, we can easily leave our wives feeling used and manipulated. After all, we have done all this work and put on our best behavior all day to get them into the bedroom in the first place. We only say a couple of words like "good night" and go to bed, missing an opportunity to leave a great last impression. A lot has been said about making a good first impression. The last impression may be totally underrated in life, marriage, and in business! Let me relate this to the business world for a moment. If a man wants to buy a car or make some other major purchase and the salesperson "wines 'em and dines 'em" to bring them to the point of sale only to drop them once they have signed on the dotted line, they feel used and abused. We know in business that often the difference between single or recurring sales is centered around the services rendered after the sale has been made.

What is true in business is true in the bedroom in this regard. A woman often wants to be held after sex. She may want to lie on your chest, hold hands, or have you play with her hair as you reaffirm your love for her. Softly caress your wife and tell her how much you care about her and not just her body parts! Tell her what an awesome lover and wife she is to you! Everyone needs reinforcement. If husbands would spend just five quality minutes after lovemaking, they would see a lot more action in the bedroom and make their wives feel special instead of used.

> ৪০০৪
>
> SOFTLY CARESS YOUR WIFE AND TELL HER HOW MUCH YOU CARE ABOUT HER AND NOT JUST HER BODY PARTS!

STICKING POINTS

❖ Would your wife say you are a "deadhead" after sex?

❖ Make a point to spend a quality amount of time cuddling, talking, and enjoying the "afterglow" of love with your spouse.

WOMEN
STICKING SEXUALLY

CHAPTER THIRTY-FOUR

Don't Make Your Husband Beg for Sex

Give freely and spontaneously.
Don't have a stingy heart.

Deuteronomy 15:10 (The Message)

No man wants to beg for sex! No man wants to beg for anything but especially when it comes to sex. Don't deflate his manhood or emasculate him by making him beg for sex. A husband feels as if he is not attractive and important to his wife when she doesn't take time to freely make love to him. A husband feels loved when his wife receives him and responds to him sexually. When a man experiences sexual rejection from his wife he shuts down emotionally and will unconsciously quit meeting his wife's emotional needs.

When we withhold sex we can seriously mess up our husband, not only emotionally but morally as well. Guard and guide your husband's sexual appetite.

Let's consider the difference in our eating appetites. Most men eat a lot more than their wives do. A man wants an appetizer, big juicy steak, a fully-loaded baked potato, and a delicious dessert for his dinner. A woman is satisfied with a little green salad and an iced tea! Wives, most of our husbands have bigger sexual appetites than we do so we need to understand and accommodate them if we want happy husbands. A wise wife realizes that if her husband is getting steak at home he is not likely to go out for a hamburger elsewhere! Since this may be the greatest perceived need your husband has, do your best to keep him fully satisfied sexually. Sex should never be reduced down to a household chore. I have heard of women who chewed gum or played with their hair while having sex. If you are bored tell him what you want, don't blow bubbles or braid your hair. If you make sex difficult for him, he will resent you and only want what he cannot have. Make it easy and he will love you and not be so caught up in the hunt all the time. Sex is an awesome gift that keeps giving. You can give it to your husband over and over again and he will not want to exchange it or return it. For over twenty-two years my husband has been counseling men who have had affairs. He says he has never heard a married man say that he was glad that he went out and had an affair. In fact over and over he has heard men say that they just wanted to be "consistent and creative" with their own wives. One man who had been in an affair for over five years was in my husband's office openly weeping and said that all he ever wanted was to be with his wife. She got the picture and reconciled her marriage but both of them went through a lot of needless pain.

If I am on a diet and skipping meals, as a wife and mother it doesn't mean that I won't feed my family or that I expect them to eat the same sized portions that I'm eating. Let's reverse the picture for a moment. When I am hungry and I want something to eat my husband knows to stop whether he is hungry or not. If he doesn't stop he is well aware that I will be grumpy and irritable. Ladies, think about how your husband acts if you withhold sex from him. Some husbands feel it would be easier to climb Mt. Everest than to have sex with their wives. Don't use sex as a weapon to punish him. This will only drive a wedge between the two of you.

STICKING POINTS

❖ What happens to a man when he experiences sexual rejection?

❖ Are you starving your husband's sexual appetite?

❖ If so, why and what things can you do to change that?

❖ Determine in advance within your mind and heart to be responsive to your husband when he makes an advance.

CHAPTER THIRTY-FIVE

Are Men Shallow?

Charm is deceptive, and beauty evaporates,
but a woman who has the fear of the Lord should be praised.

Proverbs 31:30 (GWT)

In the hit movie *Shallow Hal,* Jack Black could only see a woman's value based on her outward beauty. Through Tony Robbins, he is now able to see the inner beauty of women and falls in love with a very large lady! *Shallow Hal* may be a funny movie to watch, but appearance is not a laughing matter to most men. We can call men "shallow" but they have been wired to be aroused visually. How quickly we can forget that.

Let's admit it ladies, most of us went to great extremes to look our best during the "dating days" of our relationship, but rarely keep up the pace once we got our man! Once children come on the scene, it is easy to get busy and let things go downhill fast! I have five wonderful children

> ℘ℂℛ
> WE CAN CALL MEN "SHALLOW" BUT THEY HAVE BEEN WIRED TO BE AROUSED VISUALLY.

and when our last child was born, I knew I needed to get in shape and lose the extra baby fat.

My husband needed to gain weight and I needed to lose it. We made a deal with each other that he would gain fifteen pounds and I would lose fifteen pounds. The added incentive for me was my husband's challenge that whoever reached their goal first would get a new wardrobe. My husband is very, very competitive but I prevailed and got my shopping spree. In fact, I ended up losing thirty pounds and he gained thirty pounds and even though we are in our forties, we have never looked or felt better! We now work out two to three times per week together and have more energy and desire to love one another than when we were first married over twenty years ago. One of the side benefits of our "get in shape lifestyle" is that our teenage son and daughter and church staff members are now working out on a regular basis.

Looks are very important to men! Many men are surrounded by well-dressed, made up, sweet smelling women at work all day long. When they come home, what will they find? Will it be a house full of misplaced toys and a disheveled wife or a woman of their dreams? The truth is that we feel better when we have taken the time to make ourselves look better. Let him be excited about coming home to feast his eyes upon you. God has wired men in such a way that their sex drive is connected to their eyes. Let's face it, men are aroused visually whether we like it or not. In the Bible, in Song of Solomon, I found that the woman mentions her lover's appearance in eight ways: the hair, eyes, mouth, lips, hands, legs, cheek, and his head. But her lover mentions her appearance in sixteen different ways: the eyes, teeth, lips, mouth, temples, neck, tongue, hair, feet, hips, hands, navel, belly, nose, head, and of course, her breasts.

Men care about appearance at least twice as much as we do and quite frankly, appearances do matter to me and to most women. Ladies, looking sexy for men before sex is important to them. In this area you can save time and energy. It might only stay on for three minutes, but if it is important to them, why not please them? When we feel good about our bodies, we feel freer with them. Guys don't want their wives changing in the dark or hiding in a closet while changing, they want to see you! Ask your husband what he thinks looks good on you. Also ask him what he hates you to wear. Paul has banned flannel pajamas from our bedroom! When he is gone I sneak on my banned pajamas because they are so comfortable, even though they definitely don't flatter my figure.

A lot of women don't want to dress sexy for their husbands because they say that they don't feel sexy. Here is an area that you have just got to trust your husband. If it is in the privacy of your own home, take his word for it and be creative. One preacher's wife who spoke to our church ladies said it well, "If my husband wants me to dress up like a cowgirl in the bedroom, I'm going to do it." Find out what he likes and surprise him with what you wear both inside and outside the house.

The male gender's fixation with our appearance may seem shallow to us but it is the way they are wired from birth to the grave. To rewire a home is a very big ordeal and a very costly process. Instead of attempting to rewire your husband, why not get with the flow and put some electricity in your marriage by looking your very best for him.

STICKING POINTS

❖ Do you take care of yourself and your home the way you did when you first got married?

❖ What thing can you and your husband do together to get in shape, lose weight, et cetera that will help you both feel good about each other?

CHAPTER THIRTY-SIX

Have Sex with Your Husband
More Than Once a Week

I say, "I'm going to climb that palm tree! I'm going to caress its fruit!" Oh yes! Your breasts will be clusters of sweet fruit to me, Your breath clean and cool like fresh mint.

Song of Solomon 7:8 (The Message)

In the book, *The Five Love Needs of a Man and Woman*, it states that "sexual infrequency should be a cause of concern in any marriage." (By the way, the definition of sexual infrequency that the book gives is "once a week or less.")

The Bible actually teaches us that sex should be continually engaged in during all of married life except for one reason. 1 Corinthians 7:5 (NIV) says, "Do not deprive each other except by mutual consent and for a time, so that you may devote yourselves to prayer." Proverbs 31:12 (NKJV) says, "She does him good and not evil All the days of her life." I can almost guarantee your husband would consider sex a "good thing."

Some men admit that they desire sex on a daily basis and some once a month! The best source for you to find out about your husband's individual needs is to ask him. Don't rely on friends, magazine surveys, or TV talk shows, go directly to him. When we withhold sex we have the power to mess up our husbands emotionally and spiritually. The number one need given by more husbands than any other is their sexual need. No surprise!

> ℘℩
> THE BEST SOURCE FOR YOU TO FIND OUT ABOUT YOUR HUSBAND'S INDIVIDUAL NEEDS IS TO ASK HIM.

In the vast majority of cases a husband's overall rating of his marriage will not be far off from his rating of his sex life. It is not just that he wants quality, but he wants quantity as well. You may be waiting for the right moment, while he is revved up and ready to go on a moments notice! Pleasing your husband sexually requires scheduling sex and also spontaneity, not just doing it when all the atmospheric conditions are perfectly lined up. Get a lock on your bedroom door and don't hesitate to use it day or night! Sex during naptime or while the kid's are watching a video during the day may work out better for both of your energy levels.

Sex will not only make your husband happy but it may very well make both of you healthier. The secret of the Fountain of Youth may be more sex! In his book, *Sheet Music*, Dr. Kevin Leman writes, "David Weeks, a neuropsychologist at Royal Edinburgh Hospital in Scotland suggests that more orgasms may lead to a greater release of hormones that bolster your immune system and slow premature aging. This was in response to a ten-year study of more than 3,500 men and women. Those who looked the youngest reported far more active sex lives than the older looking participants."

How we feel about ourselves affects how we actually begin to look. When you engage in regular sexual relations, that very act affirms your body, because your husband is loving it, adoring it, and caressing it. Do everything you can to make yourself feel and look physically attractive to your husband. When you feel sexy to him you will be much more prone to desire sex. I know women who dress in the dark because they are so self-conscious of the way they look. If your husband wants to turn off the lights when you undress you definitely have a problem! Make your best effort to work on what God has given you, and let him love your body.

One husband told me that his wife was a "hottie." When I saw her, I almost had to laugh. She is not a conventional beauty. In fact, in many ways you could even say that nature has not been kind to her. But you would never convince her husband of many years of that. Why? He says that she wears him out in bed. She can't get enough of him and he can't get enough of her. The average man might look at her and see a homely face and an unbecoming body, but her husband sees a woman he has enjoyed, delighted in, and in every way adored. Frequent sex with a person can literally change how he or she looks at you. Proverbs 23:7 (NASB) says, "For as he thinks within himself, so he is."

In the magazine, *Redbook*, March 2001 issue, it states that studies have shown that lovemaking elevates the levels of brain chemicals associated with desire. So the best way to increase your yearning for sex is to have it more often.

Sticking Points

❖ What does frequent sex do to a man?

❖ What does the Bible teach us about sex?

❖ List three things you can do practically to increase the frequency of sex between you and your husband.

1._____

2._____

3._____

CHAPTER THIRTY-SEVEN

Initiate Sex with Your Husband

*Flood waters can't drown love. . . . Love can't be bought,
love can't be sold—it's not to be found in the marketplace.*

Song of Solomon 8:7 (The Message)

Many people get bored in the bedroom because they lack creativity and spontaneity. If the same partner always initiates sex and you are always in the same place and in the same position you are headed for boredom in the bedroom if you are not already there. The saying goes "it takes two to tango" and it takes two to have a happy, healthy sex life.

> ℅℃℞
> MANY PEOPLE GET BORED IN THE BEDROOM BECAUSE THEY LACK CREATIVITY AND SPONTANEITY.

Years ago my husband counseled a man whose wife put up with sex. She would literally play with her hair and chew gum while he attempted to make love to her. He ended up in an affair and came to my husband for help. He didn't want anyone else; he only wanted his wife to contribute towards their love life.

One of the ways a wife can contribute to her and her husband's love life is by initiating sex. A husband wants and needs his wife to do this for him to feel that he is desirable to his wife. This is no small deal! It is a big turnon for him and it helps make your marriage more of a partnership. Sex is a two-way street!

When you initiate sex you are in the driver's seat and can steer your husband in the direction that you want to go. Too many women think that sex is just for the man, so they end up resenting sex and seeing it as their duty to just show up and go along for the ride. Women who initiate sex will often also find the courage to make it work for both partners. God has intended for sex to be mutually enjoyable so it is important to communicate and act on your own needs and desires.

Talk sex with your husband! You can't get great in the bedroom without talking about it. Don't just talk about sex annually, but discuss what you like and don't like in your sex life. Dr. Kevin Leman states that in his practice he has found most couples spend 99.9 percent of their sexual relationship making love and .1 percent talking about it. Talking about it will help you to grow and develop your love life.

Talk about sex to find one another's hot and cold spots and what atmosphere each partner wants when engaging in lovemaking. The more you talk the more you will discover each other's sexual goals and strategies. Your mind-set can and should evolve to please one another and not merely gratify yourself. Just like you should have a vision for your life, business, career, marriage, and family you should have a vision of what you see for your sex life.

In the Bible, Ezekiel had a vision of a valley filled with a bunch of dry bones. God instructed Ezekiel to speak life into those dried up bones. You may need to speak some words of life into your sex life. "Death and life are in the power of the tongue" Proverbs 18:21 (AMP).

Tell your husband how he attracts and satisfies you and build him up with your words for what he is doing right instead of focusing on what he is doing wrong. A husband will feel loved when his wife receives him rather than rejects him sexually. Most husbands are very satisfied just to have a willing partner when they initiate sex. If you really want to blow his mind, initiate sex with him instead of always waiting for his advances! This is a big turnon for a man and validates his masculinity.

How many times have we seen men commit adultery with women less attractive than their wives? The appeal of the seductress is not merely physical, but a man's ego is stroked and he is emotionally touched when a woman wants to make love to him. It is not only okay, it is highly advisable for you to seduce your husband from time to time. Why should you leave the door open for your husband's ego to be stroked by another woman? I have decided to give my husband all the sexual attention that he needs and in so doing I am helping cut off sexual temptation from his life. This is a great way to help affair-proof your marriage. We can be great helpmates to our husbands just by initiating sex and letting them know that they've still got what it takes!

STICKING POINTS

❖ What is one way a wife can contribute to her and her husband's love life?

❖ By initiating sex, what will happen to your husband's ego?

❖ Take time to talk to your husband about ways you both can improve your sex life.

CHAPTER THIRTY-EIGHT

Let Him Know That You Enjoy Having Sex with Him

A threefold cord is not quickly broken.

Ecclesiastes 4:12 (AMP)

A husband gets discouraged when his wife does not express her passion for him. The fact is that a man finds much of his own masculinity in his sexuality. In the book *The Five Love Needs of Men and Women* by Dr. Gary and Barbara Rosberg, they state, "Although percentages differ from man to man, no less than 50 percent and up to 90 percent of a man's self-image, his 'feeling like a man' is locked up in his sexuality. Sex, passion, pleasing the woman he loves, that's what makes a man feel like a man." Making love to him may be one of the fastest ways to boost your husband's self-image and his self-confidence.

I heard a story of a man who was a public school teacher and even though he felt his job was important, he was often discouraged about the amount of money he was earning. His wife noticed his recurring depression on paydays and she decided to do something about it. She validated him with her words of encouragement and made love to him on payday.

We go to the chiropractor to get an adjustment on our spines to keep us healthy and happy. Sometimes a wife wonders why her husband's attitude has grown cold towards her. What your husband needs may not be a motivational message from Zig Ziglar but a little "show and tell" from you! When you both "show him" and "tell him" that you enjoy making love to him on a consistent basis you may just send his attitude through the roof! Let's face it, husbands receive an "attitude adjustment" when they are passionately made love to and it keeps your marriage healthy and happy.

Sex is God's wedding gift to us. It does not wear out like other wedding gifts you receive, like sheets, toasters, irons, towels, et cetera. Because it is a gift from above, it is good and should be getting better all the time. If you don't like sex, you are missing out on God's gift to you. You are telling God you don't like His gift. Marriage is work! It takes a lot of hard work to have a great marriage. It also takes a lot of hard work to have a great sex life. A great sex life requires planning. Life is busy and packed with many activities that drain us physically.

&)CR

SEX IS GOD'S WEDDING GIFT TO US.

We did a survey among over fifty couples from our church and found that one of the main reasons women didn't have more sex with their husbands was due to lack of energy. You can't expend all your energy at work or with the kids and think that sex is going to be hot with your husband. "Save yourself" for your husband. I know that there are tremendous demands placed upon modern-day women. I have five kids at home and I work part time outside of the home as well. As mothers, we often focus ourselves on attempting to meet all our children's emotional needs. Your husband also has emotional and physical needs that should not be neglected for the children or anyone else.

When we get married we make vows to love our husbands until death do us part, not until children come along. I often hear mothers of small children say that they are too tired or lack time for sex because of all the demands of child rearing. After my last child was born, the workout my husband and I decided to do not only increased my energy and my sex appeal, but also my appeal for sex. I highly recommend getting on a regular exercise program because it will help you feel better about yourself. When we feel better about ourselves we will be able to give ourselves to our husbands more freely.

A great sex life requires planning. Flirt with your husband and build up his ego! Men want to be wanted and you can really "play up" your love life by playfully touching and talking to each other. Sometimes in private you may choose to show him a little more skin than you ever would in public. Whisper in his ear and nibble on his earlobe! Tell him what a great lover he is and that you want him! Put love notes in special places that let him know he is your forever lover. Tell him that you love making love to him often, using as many different means of communication as you can.

Believe it or not, praying together on a regular basis will add a whole new dimension to your sex life. We become spiritually intimate with those we pray with and as human beings we have been created as triune beings. Connecting with your spouse in body, soul, and spirit is a triple cord of love that cannot be easily broken.

We have all heard the saying, "Good, better, best; never let it rest, till your good becomes better and your better becomes best." Sex on the physical level only is good. Sex with your soul mate is even better, but with your spiritually-bonded soul mate, it is the best.

God made sex for us to enjoy on all three levels: body, soul, and spirit. As you take your sex life to the next level you will be more bonded with your husband and him with you! Sex may be work, but it shouldn't be a chore and as you learn to better love your husband, make sure to let him know you are enjoying the journey!

STICKING POINTS

❖ What things make a man feel like a man?

❖ What does a great sex life require?

❖ Try two creative things this week to spruce up your sex life with your spouse.

MEN
STICKING SPIRITUALLY

CHAPTER THIRTY-NINE

Lay Hands on Her and Pray for Her

Isaac prayed to the LORD on behalf of his wife, because she was barren; and the LORD answered him and Rebekah his wife conceived.

Genesis 25:21 (NASB)

Let's admit it men, when we think of laying hands on our wives the first thing that comes to mind is not spiritual blessing and impartation. God has called men to headship in the home and leadership in the church community. This starts by our taking our spiritual authority seriously. It's interesting to note that even though Eve ate the forbidden fruit first, God called Adam on the carpet and not Eve. Why? Simply because God had told Adam not to eat of the fruit and He expected Adam to tell Eve not to partake since he was the spiritual head of his house.

God gave Adam and all men three primary responsibilities in the home: to guard, guide, and govern.

God wants husbands to guard their wives, not only from physical danger but spiritual danger as well. It begins with husbands praying for and with their wives. Prayer bonds you with your spouse and helps provide security, which is one of the basic needs of most women. You will become intimate with whomever you pray with. It only makes sense to pray with your wife.

True story: One husband was complaining about the lack of physical intimacy in his marriage. After being implored to pray with his wife, he took up the challenge and later reported that his intimacy problem was resolved.

> ೫ೲ
> IT IS VITALLY IMPORTANT THAT WE ARE FOLLOWING HIS DIRECTIONS SO WE CAN SPIRITUALLY LEAD OUR WIVES AND FAMILIES.

Husbands, guiding our wives implies that we know where we are going ourselves. As a spiritual guide you need a map (the Word of God) and a compass (a working relationship with the Holy Spirit) to get to the right destination. When we get alone with the Lord and open the Bible it is amazing how God can direct our steps. The Bible says, "The steps of a *good* man are ordered by the Lord" (Psalm 37:23 NKJV).

Where God guides He provides. It is vitally important that we are following His directions so we can spiritually lead our wives and families. I highly suggest getting involved with a men's Bible study group or at least reading some Promise Keeper's books to give you the necessary tools for building a marriage and family that will last a lifetime.

As head of the household, a man is to govern his family by receiving input from all family members and then making the major decisions. We have plenty of dysfunctional families in America, where the kids rule the roost. The Hollywood version of most fathers is a busy, bumbling bozo of a man who is totally out of touch with what is going on in their own home. He is the last to know and the slowest to catch on. Men, we are to be servant leaders who always have the family's best interest in mind. When we truly are servant leaders our wives and kids won't resent but rather respect our leadership. Too many men forfeit their God-given leadership role to their wives or even to their children. Jesus said the greatest among us is the servant of all and His ultimate act of service was when He died for us.

The patriarchs of old laid hands upon family members and transferred spiritual blessings from one generation to the next. A husband who is a loving servant leader will bless his wife, his own life, and create a model of marriage that his children and grandchildren can follow. A man's greatest need is to obtain significance. On their death bed no one says, "I wish I would have spent more time in the office, made more money, or worked more hours." They often regret having short-changed their wives and families and suffered the loss of relationship for it.

As we love and serve our wives, we are not just investing in our marriage but we are setting an example for our children and their future spouses to follow.

STICKING POINTS

❖ When was the last time you prayed, I mean really prayed, for your wife?

❖ Before your wife's day begins, take the time to pray for her! Take it to the next level by being an example and do it in front of the kids.

CHAPTER FORTY

Start a Storehouse

The LORD *will command the blessing on you*
in your storehouses and in all
to which . . . the LORD *your God is giving you.*

Deuteronomy 28:8 (NKJV)

Security is a major issue for most women. By far the most difficult time in our marriage was not when I bought Patti a badminton set and toaster for her birthday but when we had accumulated a lot of debt. It was during this time that one day Patti packed her suitcase and was literally headed out the door. It is so pitiful to see a grown man beg, but I did. I begged her not to leave and thank God she didn't. I realized that I had to change my spending and saving habits if I was going to provide a safe and secure environment for my wife.

Many young couples today start out their marriages deeply in debt and allow the "plastic fantastic" to undermine the peace and stability of their marriages. Every marriage needs to have a budget, or what I call a financial game plan to better manage their money, and subsequently, their stress load. God told His people in Deuteronomy 28:8 that He would command His blessing on them in their storehouses. A storehouse is a place of savings or a system of wealth accumulation. The truth is your earning power will never equal your yearning power! We live in a society that believes in instant gratification instead of delayed gratification. It is this mindset that has taken its toll on many marriages.

The Storehouse Principle is based upon three truths:

+ There will be rotating cycles of prosperity and recession in every economy.
+ Prosperous times are times to save and store away wealth.
+ When recession hits, former surpluses can be used to meet needs and to multiply wealth through acquiring assets sold by others (without storehouses) for pennies on the dollar.

In the Bible, Joseph saved up 20 percent of the nation of Egypt's resources for seven prosperous years. He was then able to save himself, his family, and the nation during the next seven years of severe famine (see Genesis 41 and 47).

&)&

A MONTHLY SAVINGS PLAN CAN LITERALLY SAVE YOUR MARRIAGE FROM A FINANCIAL CATASTROPHE.

A monthly savings plan can literally save your marriage from a financial catastrophe. After talking about the Storehouse Principle in a recent church service, I had a middle-aged man approach me. He told me that he started a storehouse saving plan when he was younger and that it literally sustained him for two years of unexpected unemployment.

Implementing a storehouse saving plan may create a little stress on your marriage and finances now, but if it is done properly it will save you a lot stress later. Joseph saved 20 percent of the income he was managing in very prosperous times. Maybe you can only manage to save 10 percent, 5 percent, or even 2 percent but every little bit will help to create peace and stability in your life and in your home. Couples with a storehouse don't stress out over a roof leak, a broken down washing machine, or a new set of tires for their car.

There are many ways you can set up a storehouse including opening up a savings account, investing in mutual funds, buying real estate/rental property, or even starting a side business. The average American has no more than two months of savings in the bank at one time and often carries that amount of credit card debt alone.

I say—the couple that saves together stays together! Having a storehouse of savings really does help to keep couples more emotionally healthy and happy with their lives and marriages. A storehouse is a financial foundation that can help build a marriage that can withstand the inevitable financial storms that come to every house. Husbands that lead the way by disciplining themselves financially to save and invest create a safe and secure environment for their marriages to thrive and not just survive.

STICKING POINTS

❖ Do you have any storehouses set up?

❖ Make a goal of reading the book *Storehouse Principle* by Van Crouch and setting up a new storehouse this year.

WOMEN
Sticking Spiritually

CHAPTER FORTY-ONE

Marry His Dream

*Do two people walk hand in hand
if they aren't going to the same place?*

Amos 3:3 (The Message)

When a woman marries a man she should also marry his dream! We all know of someone who lost their dream the day they got married. Some quit college, some gave up a career, a business, or a dream of building a family. What is your dream? What is your husband's dream? Spouses should be dream makers, not dream takers. Before I married Paul we had many deep conversations to make sure that we were going to be striving for the same goals and dreams in this short life. Paul's dream was to fulfill his call in full-time ministry. He said this call could take us to foreign lands with less-than-attractive living conditions. He also stated that we might have to move a lot in order to follow his ministry dream. We never had to live in a third world country but we did move eight times in ten years! Before anyone gets married they need to pass the dream test!

Take the "Dream Test":

- ◆ Do you know your spouse's dream in life well enough to be able to explain it in detail to your spouse and others?
- ◆ Does your spouse know your dream well enough to be able to explain it in detail to you and others?
- ◆ Do you believe in each other's dreams?
- ◆ Do you have an action plan (preferably in writing) to help you fulfill your dreams?
- ◆ Are you willing to make significant contributions and sacrifices towards your spouse's dream?

There are two types of individuals we can marry: dreamers or doubters. Dreamers build every day around their dream; doubters waste every day around their excuses. Dreamers discover their future by discovering their gifts; doubters discourage their future by discovering their handicaps. Dreamers see opposition as a window; doubters see opposition as a wall. If you are a dreamer, make sure you marry someone who has a dream.

Building your life's dream is a lot like building a dream house. In 2001, Paul and I built our dream house on a golf course with a lovely lake behind us.

1. We first had to select a piece of property that had the size and setting we desired. Dream big but don't make your dreams unrealistic and impossible to achieve.

2. Next, select a builder that you are confident can get the job done. Jesus Christ is a dream builder, and He specializes in building dreams and building lives.

3. Then you need to have a blueprint. The best dreams are worthless without a plan. Blueprints give you the ability to see both the big picture and the small details.

4. As the house goes up you will have to enlist many different tradesmen (specialists) to help you in their area of expertise. Dreams worth living will require many mentors to help you go to the next level in life.

5. Communication between spouses is essential as the dream house takes form. Hundreds of decisions must be made. Without communication and agreement this can be a very grievous process. Our lawyer encouraged us not to build a dream house together because he said that it causes marital stress and even divorce between couples. We avoided traumatizing our marriage by constantly keeping open our communication lines with each other and with our builder. Building a dream house requires sacrifice, commitment, and perseverance, as there will be many challenges along the way.

In the end, we found it was worth striving for our common goal of building a house together. When one spouse had strong feelings about some aspect of the house, the other spouse was generally quick to concede to the other's wishes. Sometimes it wasn't easy. My husband and I don't fight, but we sometimes have "intense fellowship!" For instance, in the kitchen I wanted wood floors and Paul wanted to save money with ceramic tile. It took him quite a while "to see the light." I had to make my case and do my homework. Today he is happy we decided to go with wood.

Dreams motivate us in life, and when we have compatible dreams they can be great motivators in our marriages as well. Some wives are like Joseph's brothers, constantly throwing their husband's dreams into a pit (see Genesis 37:23). Don't despise his dreams; inspire them with your words of wisdom and encouragement. As you help him pursue his dreams you will grow closer together and build a better marriage and life.

STICKING POINTS

❖ Did you marry a dreamer or a doubter?

❖ Describe a dreamer.

❖ Find two practical ways to help your husband achieve his dreams.

1._____

2._____

CHAPTER FORTY-TWO

Pray for Your Husband

*Pray for each other so that you can
live together whole and healed.
The prayer of a person living right with God
is something powerful to be reckoned with.*

James 5:16 (The Message)

According to a survey conducted by Lutheran Brotherhood of Minneapolis, nine out of ten Americans say they pray. Nearly all of those surveyed said that they pray for their families and six out of ten said that they also pray for their enemies. Sometimes when we pray for our husbands we may feel like we are praying for the enemy. When we pray, it shouldn't be based on our feelings but based on our faith in a prayer answering God! I have found that God has answered my prayers over and over again through the various stages of life that I have passed through! As a teenager I prayed, "Oh God, you have to get me a husband," and He did! As a newly married young lady I prayed, "Oh God, you have to give me children," and He did! Now at times I pray, "Oh God, you have to save me from this husband and these five children that you gave me."

Many times we all spend too much time praying for ourselves instead of those closest to us. There is no closer human relationship than the marriage relationship and this is a great place to focus your faith and practice your prayers!

Start your prayers by praying for God's will to be done in your life as well as that of your husband's. Let me tell you about the "Other Person" in your marriage. A Christian marriage includes more than just a husband and a wife. That other person is God! In our solar system the sun is the center with the Earth rotating around it. To have a truly blessed marriage we must have God in the center of our universe. The husband and wife also have a big "pull" on one another's life and whatever happens to one will directly affect the other. A praying wife can greatly influence her husband and indirectly affect the health and strength of their relationship together. Prayer helps to insulate your love and marriage from dangerous outside influences. Yes, you will still go through hot and cold times, but prayer softens the blow and strengthens your resolve to get through whatever you need to get through.

Marriage is a great place to pray the prayer of agreement. In Matthew 18:19 (NIV) Jesus said, "Again, I tell you that if two of you on earth agree about anything you ask for, it will be done for you by my Father in heaven." The Greek word for agreement in this verse means to "harmonize or symphonize." The place of agreement is the place of power. When we pray together we don't just add to our prayer abilities, we multiply them. Let's face it, there are numerous battles we have to face as married couples. The Bible says, "Though one may be overpowered by another, two can withstand him. And a threefold cord is not quickly broken." (Ecclesiastes 4:12 NKJV). When you pray for your husband you are unleashing God's will and God's best into your marriage. Never underestimate the power of a praying wife.

My husband has a lot of daily pressures on him as the senior pastor of our growing church of over twelve hundred people. Our church has helped to start over two dozen churches and gone through two major building programs. On top of all that, he has a children's ministry at home with five kids. I regularly pray for God's wisdom and strength for Paul and I am always on standby whenever he needs me. Back when we were building our church's original Family Ministry Center, Paul would sometimes ask me to lay hands on him and pray. He said my prayers refreshed and recharged him. He is rarely sick but whenever he is he will ask me to lay hands on him and pray for God's healing power to touch and restore him.

Marriage is a relationship that provides the possibilities of a built-in prayer partner. You don't have to pray long, flowery prayers to get started. Just designate a few minutes a day to praying for your husband and let your husband know you are praying for him. We will become intimate with those we pray for and pray with. Praying for our husband will add to our intimacy with God and our husbands.

STICKING POINTS

❖ What should your prayers be based on in praying for your husband?

❖ What can the effects be of a praying wife?

❖ Ask your husband what areas in his life he needs prayer in and start praying for him daily.

ABOUT THE AUTHORS

Paul and Patti Endrei met in Bible college and have been married for over twenty-three years. They reside in Avon, Ohio with their five children Jordan, Natasha, Gabrielle, Promise, and Gideon. In addition to their large, busy family life they have been in ministry together for over twenty-three years as well.

Pastor Paul Endrei is the senior pastor of Church on the Rise, a fast-growing interdenominational church located in a sprawling suburb of Cleveland, Ohio. He is an ordained minister and graduated from Southeastern Bible College in Lakeland, Florida with a degree in Missions. He spent seven and a half years working as a youth pastor and later as an assistant pastor at Church on the North Coast in Lorain, Ohio. In 1989, he received a Master of Arts degree in Biblical Studies from Ashland Seminary. In 2003, he received an honorary Doctor of Divinity from the National Clergy Council and The Methodist Episcopal Church.

Patti Endrei is a full-time mother of five and Pastor's wife. She attended Southeastern Bible College in Lakeland, Florida where she met Paul Endrei. In 1983 they were married and began full-time ministry together. They began their ministry as youth pastors in Lakewood, Ohio where they saw hundreds of teens come to know Christ through their ministry. Patti heads up the Women's Ministry of Church on the Rise and assists Paul in every way she can with the ministry of the church.

Pastor Paul and his wife, Patti, launched Church on the Rise in Westlake, Ohio with a vision of seeing "A Church for the Whole Family." Since the first service in 1993, the church has grown to more than 1,200 people. Pastor Paul has led Church on the Rise in the purchase of nearly 20 acres of prime land in Westlake where the church's 750-seat First Phase Family Ministry Center is located. Through a mighty series of miracles, the nearly $1 million of land was completely paid for in 6 months. The Second Phase 24,000-square-foot Community Youth Center opened in 2006.

Paul Endrei is a dynamic preacher of the gospel, conducting overseas ministries with the late Dr. Ed Cole of Promise Keepers and many others. He believes wholeheartedly in "Total Success" as God's plan for the total man and the total woman. Often Pastor Paul is called upon by various media news outlets in the Cleveland area and nationally to give a Christian perspective on issues facing our society. He has traveled extensively in all fifty states and in over twenty countries. Most recently, Pastor Paul ministered with Dr. Charles Blair in Ethiopia, and has helped to plant one thousand churches along the Ethiopian border with Sudan. He has also ministered in South Africa with Every Home for Christ Ministry.

Author Contact Information

For speaking engagements or to write to us, please use the following addresses and/or phone number:

Pastor Paul and Patti Endrei
Church on the Rise
3550 Crocker Road
Westlake, OH 44145
Phone: (440) 808-0200
Fax: (440) 808-0202
E-mail: cor@churchontherise.net

To learn more about Pastor Paul and Patti Endrei and/or order additional helpful materials for your marriage and family visit **www.churchontherise.net**